# THE
# INTERCESSOR'S
# DICTIONARY:
## *Words & Phrases*

## TERRI J. DAVIS

www.TrueVinePublishing.org

The Intercessor's Dictionary: Words and Phrases
By: Terri J. Davis

Published by: True Vine Publishing Co.
801 Dominican Dr.
Nashville, TN. 37228
www.TrueVinePublishing.org

ISBN: 978-1-962783-82-8 Paperback
ISBN: 978-1-962783-41-5 eBook

Edited by: KWAYS
Tanae Murdic
Whites Creek, TN
knightwriter@rocketmail.com

*Scripture references marked KJV are from the King James Version of the Holy Bible.*

*Scripture references marked NKJV are taken from the New King James Version®. Copyright © 1982 by Thomas Nelson. Used by permission. All rights reserved.*

*Scripture references marked NIV are from the Holy Bible, New International Version®, NIV® Copyright © 1973, 1978, 1984, 2011 by Biblica, Inc. ® Used by permission. All rights reserved worldwide.*

This book is dedicated to those who have imparted wisdom and sound teaching into me throughout my journey of life. May Heaven smile upon you.

In loving memory of my grandparents:
*Pastor Cleophas "Mr. Bible" & Estella Hall, Sr.*

*Bishop H. Jenkins Bell*

*To my family, close and extended. Thank you.*

# CONTENTS

# FOREWORD

Prayer is one of the most serious activities that a person could ever engage in. Luke 18:1 records that Jesus, our Lord Himself, taught His disciples that, "It is necessary for them to always pray and not lose heart". They followed His admonishment, which fueled their life-changing ministry and remarkable furtherance of the Gospel and the message of the kingdom beyond Jerusalem. From across the earth, the incense of prayer continues to be offered unto the Lord by born-again believers as a practice of their faith, as well as those called to intercession as their kingdom vocation. In either case, one's desire should be aimed at making an impact in the affairs of humanity through the power of prayer. To do this, a righteous person must, "Pray fervently *and* effectually, according to James 5:16 (KJV, emphasis added). Both elements are required. Sincerity and intensity do not help us hit the mark of powerful prayer. Therefore, we must seek to gain understanding and use the tools that help us make the kind of prayer that yields outcomes consistent with God's heart, will, and intentions.

In my work as a pastor and as a teacher on intercession over the last ten years, I have come across individuals who have upheld Jesus' instruction to always pray, but expressed they had, in essence, lost heart, because they were unsure if they had been praying "the right way." Job 22:27 states, "You will *make* your prayer to Him and He will hear you (ONM, emphasis added)." The word *"make"* suggests a constructional component to prayer. Any credible construction manager will tell you that a successful project involves clear blueprints and a capable team that knows how to read them then execute accordingly. Comparatively, God's word provides the blueprint for prayer, but many have fallen short in understanding and execution.

Since prayer is most simplistically defined as "communication with God", we must consider the importance of vocabulary. Proper vocabulary invokes God's character and nature within the scope of the matters we pray about. Now, let us be clear. This does not substantiate an idea that the "right" words constitute effectual prayer. The focus, rather, is to enforce the Almighty's supremacy as the One True Living God in all affairs concerning mankind. Since God bestowed upon us governing authority (dominion) over the earth, we must now grant Him the legal right to release His power in the natural realm. Through prayer, we, indeed, play an active role in the establishment of God's kingdom here and His will being done as it is in heaven (Matt. 6:10). It is imperative to add to our understanding of prayer as much as possible. While there is no shortage of resources relating to this subject matter, the key is to connect with resources that are consistent with Biblical principles and simplistic in approach to incite zeal and promote maturity. I believe that this book is such a tool.

Inspired by the Holy Spirit and written from a heart of compassion for God's people, *The Intercessor's Dictionary: Words and Phrases* is a convergence of the divine and the practical that helps crack the "code" to effectual prayer that some Christians tend to think exists. Prophetess Terri Davis debunks such a notion by comprising a catalog of terminology that will reaffirm the reader's commission in God's army, empower them to recognize that prayer is our posture in partnership with God, and help them employ winning strategies in warfare. Moreover, these scripturally-based entries give insight to God's character and nature – which must be the pith of the intercessor's fortitude and resolve. In short, this manual can elevate your understanding and execution of the blueprint for powerful prayer.

Whether you are just beginning your prayer walk or have become a seasoned prayer warrior, *The Intercessor's Dictionary: Words and Phrases* will build your confidence and competence. It is my hope that you will take full advantage of this blessing to the Body of Christ. May it not become just another book on your shelf, but a handy utility. May it become a part of your arsenal to win every battle against Satan and the demonic forces in concert with him. May it nourish your relationship with God and your sense of servitude to actively to birth His will in the earth.

Thank you, Prophetess Terri, for your contribution to help us efficiently do our part through prayer!

Apostle LaTonya R. Hite
*Founder*, Chadad Global Ministries
School of Intercession
*President*, Lifeline Prayer Network

# INTRODUCTION

In the intricate tapestry of Christian faith, prayer serves as the golden thread that binds Believers to the heart of God. It is through prayer that we commune with God—expressing our deepest longings—and partake in the unfolding of God's will in our lives and in the world around us. Intercessory prayer, particularly, holds a special place in the hearts of Believers—a sacred duty and a profound privilege bestowed upon us to stand in the gap for others and to usher in God's kingdom through our petitions.

Welcome to *The Intercessor's Dictionary: Words & Phrases.* Within the pages of this book, we embark on a journey into the depths of prayer, exploring its multifaceted dimensions, unraveling its mysteries, and equipping ourselves with the tools necessary to engage in powerful and effective intercession.

This dictionary is not merely a compilation of words and definitions; it is a roadmap for the soul—a guide that will lead you through the vast terrain of prayer, illuminating the path with insights, scriptures, and practical wisdom. Whether you are a seasoned prayer warrior or a novice in the art of intercession, this resource is designed to enrich your prayer life, deepen your understanding of prayer terminology, and empower you to pray with confidence, consistency, and faith.

As you journey through these pages, you will encounter a treasure trove of prayer terms, each accompanied by a concise definition and relevant scriptures, along with the names of God and weapons of warfare. From foundational concepts such as *faith, persistence,* and *praying in the Spirit*, to more nuanced terms like *time waster, quicken,* and *divine timing*, this dictionary covers a broad spectrum of prayer terminology that is commonly used.

Moreover, interspersed throughout the entries are reflections, prayers, and meditations that will inspire and uplift your spirit, guiding you deeper into the heart of prayer and fostering a deeper intimacy with the Holy Spirit. May this dictionary serve as a faithful companion on your journey of prayer—a companion that will strengthen your faith, ignite your passion for intercession, and empower you to believe God by faith, knowing that your prayers are heard and will be answered in due time.

While embarking on this sacred pilgrimage (a journey into the transformative power of prayer), may every word uttered become a conduit for grace, power, authority, and victory, which will lift your heart in intercession and aid in your becoming more of a vessel for God's love and mercy to flow freely into the world. Never forget that prayer is an act of love. Now, let's bust the devil's head!

*Terri Jo*

# FORMAT FOR PRAYER

Adoration & Acknowledge
    Confession & Repentance
        Thanksgiving
            Supplication
                Praise
                    Worship
                        Listening
                            Soak

Write or audio record what the Lord says or shows you.

# LAWS OF PRAYER

A law is the system of rules which a particular country or community recognizes as regulating the actions of its members and which it may enforce by the imposition of penalties. A rule defining correct procedure or behavior in a sport.

1. *Thou shall be naked before the Lord. Genesis 2:25*
2. *Thou shall be clean before the Lord. Psalm 24:3-6*
3. *Thou shall be connected to the Vine and accept the pruning of the Gardner. John 15:1-8*
4. *Thou shall agree with God's plan and word. Matthew 18:19-20*
5. *Thou shall pray in the Spirit. Jude 1:20*
6. *Thou shall believe God heard you and will answer. Proverbs 15:29; Matthew 21:22*
7. *Thou shall pray with understanding. 1 Corinthians 14:15*
8. *Thou shall decree the word of God and watch God work. Job 22:28*

# Prayer is an Assignment.

# SECTION I: PRAYING THE NAMES OF GOD

**Abba:** "Father" or "Daddy." This name of God requires intimacy. *(Mark 14:36; Romans 8:15; 2 Corinthians 6:18; Galatians 4:6)*

**Adoni:** "Lord" or "Master"; when you submit to Him as God—Adoni (Lord and Master)—you are coming to His throne with a renewed awe of His greatness. God desires for you to submit to Him, learn of His ways, and take His yoke upon you. *(Psalm 16:2; Matthew 11:25; 1 John 1:9)*

**Alpha and Omega, the:** "Beginning and End," "First and Last"—the One who was, who is, and who is to come. He *is* your all-sufficient God who will complete His good work in you. *(Revelation 22:13)*

**Attiyq Youm:** "Ancient of Days"; "Remember the former things of old: for I am God, and there is none else; I am God, and there is none like me, declaring the end from the beginning, and from ancient times the things that are not yet done, saying, My counsel shall stand, and I will do all my pleasure" *(Isaiah 46:9-10, KJV)*.

**El Chuwl:** "the God who gave you birth." In Isaiah 43, God was saying to His people, "I brought you into being and I will bring you through whatever you face." In Hebrew, this also means "to whirl, dance, writhe, fear, tremble, travail, to be in anguish, be pained"; depending on the context, it is used concerning birthing. *(Isaiah 43:1-3)*

**El Deah:** "the God of Knowledge." God *is* the God of all knowledge. God inhabits eternity. God sees the beginning, the middle, and the end. God *is* all-knowing—He can't learn anything. Nothing takes God by surprise. God *is* omniscient. *(1 Samuel 2:3; Romans 11:33-36; 1 Corinthians 1:18-31)*

**Elohim:** He has no beginning and no end. He *is* the Everlasting God or the Eternal God. *(Genesis 1:1; 21:32-33; Exodus 3:1)*

**El Elyon:** the "Most High" God. God *is* supreme. He deserves all our focus, worship, and praise—He who fulfills His purpose for you. *(Psalm 57:2; 92:1-3; Isaiah 55:8-9)*

**El Kanna:** "consuming fire, jealous God." This name contains a holy version of jealousy that God has for His people. God *is* jealous for you and me. We are greatly loved and treasured by Him. *(Exodus 34:14; Deuteronomy 6:15)*

**El Olam:** The Everlasting God or the Eternal God. *(Genesis 21:33; Isaiah 26:3 -4; 40:28; Revelation 4:8)*

**El Roi:** "the God who sees me"; He's our Shepherd, the One who watches over us day and night, feeding us and guiding us on the path of righteousness. *(Genesis 16:14-15; Psalm 23:1; John 10:11, 14-15)*

**El Sali:** "the Lord *is* my strength"; *God, my rock*—the God who *is* the strength of our hearts. He will fill us with joy and courage. *(Psalm 18:1)*

**El Shaddai:** "the All-sufficient One"—God Almighty. He has everything that we need to sustain us. *(Genesis 17:1-2; 35:11; Exodus 6:3)*

**Esh Okhlah:** "God *is* a Consuming Fire"; The Hebrew word *kaesh* ("consuming fire") is a metaphor for passion. As Jeremiah was voicing his complaint to God, God allowed him to enter His heart and feel His passion. *"Therefore, understand today that the LORD your God is He who goes over before you as a consuming fire. He will destroy them and bring them down before you; so, you shall drive them out and destroy them quickly, as the LORD has said to you"* (Deuteronomy 9:3, NKJV). *(Exodus 24:17; Isaiah 29:6; Hebrews 12:29)*

**Ish:** your "husband." God *is* the perfect husband, the One who provides protection, has endless patience, and will never divorce you no matter how unfaithful you are. *(Hosea 2:16-20; Isaiah 54:5)*

**Jehovah Hoseenu:** "the Lord, our Maker," He who creates something out of nothing; the Lord transforms His creation to His desire. He *is* the Master Potter, and we are the clay. *(Psalm 95; Isaiah 64:8; Romans 8:29; 2 Corinthians 5:17; Ephesians 2:10)*

**Jehovah Hoshiah:** God *is* our rescuer in times of distress, and we can call upon Him for help and salvation. This highlights God's saving power and His ability to deliver us from our troubles. *(Psalm 30; 71; Jude 23)*

**Jehovah Magen:** "the Lord *is* my shield, my protector." God *is* our shield. He surrounds and protects us when trouble is near. *(Psalm 3:3; 18:2; 28:7)*

**Jehovah Gibbor:** "the Lord *is* strong and mighty in battle." We must trust that the Lord is fighting for us and has already defeated our enemy—but we must allow Him to take the lead as Commander-in-Chief. God is a man of war. *(Exodus 14:13-14; Joshua 23:10; Psalm 24:8; Isaiah 10:20)*

**Jehovah Nissi:** "the Lord *is* my banner." His name is to be lifted high where we and the enemy can see it as a reminder of His security, hope, and freedom. He fights every battle for us. The Lord *is* our miracle. *(Exodus 17:15; Psalm 20:1, 4-5)*

**Jehovah Rapha:** "the Lord who heals." God *is* our Healer—in body, soul, and spirit; to mend, repair, or restore something to its normal or useful state. *(Exodus 15:26; Psalm 107:20; 147:3; Matthew 4:23; Mark 1:40)*

**Jehovah Sabaoth:** refers to His sovereignty over all the powers of the universe, natural and supernatural. God *is* LORD of Hosts—God of the heavenly armies, and the army of Israel. It is a royal title of great power. *(1 Samuel 17:45; Isaiah 6:3; Psalm 46:7)*

**Jehovah Tsuri:** "The Lord *is* My Rock." God is described as a Rock throughout the books of the prophets and Ps. God is immovable, unbreakable, a safe place for retreat, and a fortress in battle! He *is* a true source of strength, a firm foundation, support, and defense. He is the solid rock on which we stand. *(2*

*Samuel 22:2-4; Psalm 18:2; 62:1-2; 1 Peter 2:4-8)*

**Kaddish:** "I will be exalted, and I will be sanctified; I will make Myself known in the eyes of many nations so that they will know that I am God." This also proclaims the greatness of God. *(Ezekiel 38:23)*

**Kadosh:** means "holy"—people, places, and things. *(Exodus 3:5; 3:15; Acts 7:33-34)*

**Lion of Judah:** the Lion of the tribe of Judah, the Root of David, has triumphed. He is able to open the scroll and its seven seals. *(Joel 3:16; Hosea 11:10; Revelation 5:5)*

**Migdal-Oz:** God, "my strong tower or stronghold." He *is* a place of strength and safety. *(Psalm 18:2, 45)*

**Qedosh Yisrael:** "Holy One of Israel"—the God whose holiness separates Him from sin and evil, but is also full of His power, knowledge, justice, mercy, goodness, and love. *(Leviticus 19:1-2; Romans 12:1-2; Hebrews 4:16)*

**Ruach HaKodesh:** the Hebrew word for "spirit, breath, or wind." When spoken, the word engages one's breath and lungs. *(Exodus 10:13; Numbers 11:31; Judges 6:34; 1 Samuel 16:14; 1 Kings 18:12; Acts 2)*

**Yahweh:** "I Am"—the Self-existent One. I Am. He was. He is. He always has been and always will be. He *is* the Self-existent One with no beginning and no end. *(Exodus 3:14-15; John 6:35; 8:12; 11:25; 15:1)*

**Yahweh Hesed:** "God of forgiveness." The Hebrew word *hesed* is often translated as "mercy, kindness, or lovingkindness." *(Nehemiah 9:17)*

**Yahweh Shalom:** "the Lord *is* peace." This peace speaks of wholeness, harmony, and completeness. Shalom is not dependent on circumstances but comes from living in harmony with God. *(Judges 6:22-24; Numbers 6:22-27; Galatians 5:22; Isaiah 26:3)*

**Yahweh Shammah:** "the LORD *is* there"; consider His compassion: God is literally in our situation—the God who *is* there in every one of our circumstances. *(Ezekiel 48:35; Luke 2:22-30; Jeremiah 29:11)*

**Yahweh Tsidkenu:** "the Lord *our* righteousness." The word *Tsidkenu* is derived from *Tsedek* and means "righteousness, honesty, accuracy, justice, truth, or integrity—One who has intervened on your behalf to restore you to His fellowship." *(Jeremiah 23:6)*

**Yahweh Tsuri:** "the Lord *is* my rock." The word "rock" represents God's permanence, His protection, and His enduring faithfulness. *(Psalm 18:2; 2 Samuel 22:2-4; Isaiah 26:3-4; 1 Peter 2:4-8)*

**Yahweh-Yireh:** "the Lord *will* provide"—the God who sees our situation beforehand and is able and willing to provide for our needs. *(Genesis 22:13-14; Matthew 14:13-21; 2 Kings 4:1-7; Hebrews 11:17-19)*

**Yahweh Zamar:** "the God who sings." God sang a song to David to cut away his *yetzer hara*—evil inclinations. When God sang to David and David sang to God (in harmony and as their voices blended), the enemy could no longer overcome David with temptation. *(Psalm 118; Zephaniah 3:17)*

**Yatsar:** to fashion, to frame; the potter; to take shape by squeezing; the One who molds, creates, and restores us to the persons He intended us to be. *(Jeremiah 1:5; 12:2-6; Psalm 139:14; Isaiah 64:8)*

**Yeshua Hamashiach:** "Jesus the Messiah"—the Anointed One. *(Matthew 7:21 -23; John 1:41; 4:25)*

# "*Prayer is an Act of Love.*"

**DR. MATTHEW STEVENSON, III**
**ALL NATIONS WORSHIP ASSEMBLY**

# SECTION II: TYPES OF PRAYERS

**Prayer of Adoration (praising God):** Prayers of adoration simply means we exalt, esteem, bless and honor the Lord. We reflect upon His character – holiness, goodness, love, mercy, power, grace, and dominion. Revelation 4:11 reads, *"You are worthy, O Lord, to receive glory and honor and power; for You created all things, and by Your will they exist and were created" (NKJV).* In essence, we are to adore the Lord because He is worthy. *"For by Him all things were created that are in heaven and that are on earth, visible and invisible, whether thrones or dominions or principalities or powers. All things were created through Him and for Him. And He is before all things, and in Him all things consist" (Colossians 1:16-17, NKJV).*

**Prayer of Supplication (asking for what we need, including forgiveness):** a prayer through which requests are made known to God—whether we are making requests known for ourselves or for other people. This requires one to repent for wrong. Philippians 4:6 reads, *"Be careful for nothing; but in every thing by prayer and supplication with thanksgiving let your requests be made known unto God"* (KJV).

**Prayer of Confession (acknowledgment and disclosure of sin):** a prayer confessing sin and asking for repentance. *"If we confess our sins, He is faithful and just to forgive us our sins and to cleanse us from all unrighteousness" (1 John 1:9, NKJV).*

**Prayer of Intercession (asking for what others need):** In Luke 23:34a, Jesus offered an intercessory prayer to God to ask for our forgiveness. He said, *"Father, forgive them; for they know not what they do"* (KJV).

**Prayer of Thanksgiving (for what God has given and done):** First Chronicles 16:34 reads, *"Give thanks to the LORD, for he is good; his love endures forever"* (NIV). Hebrews 13:15 (NRSV) states, *Through him, then, let us continually offer a sacrifice of praise to God, that is, the fruit of lips that confess his name.* First Chronicles 29:13 reads, *"Now, our God, we give you thanks, and praise your*

Terri J. Davis

*glorious name"* (NIV).

**Prayer of Salvation (receiving Jesus as Savior):** Heavenly Father, I come to You in the Name of Jesus. *Acts 2:21 (KJV)* declares that *"whosoever shall call on the name of the Lord shall be saved." Romans 10:9-10 reads, "That if thou shalt confess with thy mouth the Lord Jesus, and shalt be-lieve in thine heart that God hath raised him from the dead, thou shalt be saved.*

*For with the heart man believeth unto righteousness; and with the mouth confession is made unto salvation"* (KJV). *I receive you as my Savior of my soul and Lord over my life. Amen.*

*Prayer gives Believers the key for obtaining liberty.*

# SECTION III: WEAPONS OF WARFARE

**Aaron's Rod:** also becomes the scepter of the kings of Israel. *(Numbers 17:8)*

**Arrows:** were first made of reeds, and then of wood tipped with iron. "Arrow" is sometimes the word figuratively used for lightning *(Deuteronomy 32:23, 42; Psalm 7:13; 18:14; 144:6; Zechariah 9:14)*. They were used in war as well as in the chase *(Genesis 27:3; 49:23)*. They were also used in divination *(Ezekiel 21:21)*. Arrows are frequently employed as symbols of the following: (a) calamity or disease inflicted by God *(Job 6:4; 34:6; Psalm 38:2; Deuteronomy 32:23; Ezekiel 5:16)*; (b) some sudden danger *(Psalm 91:5)*; (c) bitter words *(Psalm 64:3)*; or (d) false testimony *(Proverbs 25:18)*.

**Axe:** used in Deuteronomy 19:5; 20:19; 1 Kings 6:7, as the translation of a Hebrew word which means "chopping." It was used for felling trees *(Isaiah 10:34)* and hewing timber for building. It is the rendering of a different word in *Judges 9:48; 1 Samuel 13:20-21; Psalm 74:5*—which refers to its sharpness *(Ezekiel 26:9)*.

**Battering Ram:** a military engine, consisting of a long beam of wood hung upon a frame, for making breaches in walls. The end of it—which was brought against the wall—was shaped like a ram's head. *(Ezekiel 4:2; 21:22)*

**Battle Axe:** a mallet or heavy war club applied metaphorically *(Jeremiah 51:20)* to Cyrus, God's instrument in destroying Babylon.

**Boomerang:** a curved, flat piece of wood that can be thrown so that it will return to the thrower; a plan or action; return to the originator, often with negative consequences. *(Isaiah 55:8-11; Romans 11:9)*

**Bow:** the main offensive weapon. The arrows were carried in a quiver, with the bow always unbent till the moment of action. *(Genesis 27:3; 48:22; Psalm 18:34)*

Terri J. Davis

**Breastplate:** used for the covering of the back and breast and both upper arms. *(Isaiah 59:17; Ephesians 6:14)*

**Bronze Bow:** the most powerful and accurate distance *weapon* of antiquity, able to shoot at about 80 meters (262 feet). The bow is capable of firing arrows that would pierce both bone and horn plate armor. The horn parts are complex in shape and require many hours of drilling, sawing, cutting, and grinding with bronze tools. Not only were the bows difficult to manufacture, but they required the specialization of labor. The wooden and horned parts of each bow would have been worked on by skilled craftsmen. *(Job 20:24; 2 Samuel 22:35; Psalm 18:34)*

**Buckler:** another word for small shield (*1 Kings 10:17; Ezekiel 26:8*). In Psalm 91:4, "buckler" is actually a roundel used by archers or slingers.

**Hammer:** a tool with a heavy metal head mounted at right angles at the end of a handle, used for jobs such as breaking things and driving in nails. *(Psalm 74:6; Isaiah 41:7; Jeremiah 23:29)*

**Helmet:** used as protection for the head, as worn by warriors. *(Ephesians 6:17)*

**Javelin:** (Hebrew: *hanith*)—a lance, from its flexibility (*1 Samuel 18:10-11; 19:9-10; 20:33*); (Hebrew: *romah*)—a lance for heavily armed troops, so called from its piercing. *(Numbers 25:7; 1 Samuel 17:45)*

**Jawbone:** A jawbone of a donkey provided Samson with a weapon for the great slaughter of the Philistines (*Judges 15:15*), in which he slew a thousand men.

**Rod of Iron:** is supposed to mean a mace or crowbar, a weapon of great power when used by a strong arm. *(Psalm 2:9)*

**Shield:** The shield was a major element of defensive armor. There was the great shield or target for the protection of the whole person. *(Genesis 15:1; Psalm 47:9; 1 Samuel 17:7; Proverbs 30:5)*

30

**Sling:** The Bible tells us that a young shepherd named David killed the giant Philistine, Goliath, with a very accurately slung stone (1 Samuel 17:40, 49). Israelites often used slings as weapons of war (2 Kings 3:25). The sling was a favorite weapon of the Benjaminites. *(1 Samuel 17:40; 1 Chronicles 12:2)*

**Spear:** another offensive weapon. *(Joshua 8:18; 1 Samuel 17:7, 45)*

**Sword:** a Hebrew sword was pointed, sometimes two-edged, worn in a sheath, and suspended from the girdle (*Exodus 32:27; 1 Samuel 31:4; 1 Chronicles 21:27; Psalm 149:6; Proverbs 5:4; Ezekiel 16:40; 21:3-5*). A sword is a symbol of divine chastisement (*Deuteronomy 32:25; Psalm 7:12; 78:62*). It is also a symbol of a slanderous tongue (*Psalm 57:4; 64:3*). There is one who speaks rashly like the thrusts of a SWORD, but the tongue of the wise brings healing (*Proverbs 12:18*). The Word of God is also likened to a sword—for the Word of God is living and active and sharper than any two-edged SWORD, and piercing as far as the division of soul and spirit, of both joints and marrow, and able to judge the thoughts and intentions of the heart (*Hebrews 4:12*).

# *Prayer requires persistence.*

**Luke 18:1-8**

# SECTION IV: DEFINITIONS & PHRASES
# A

**Abolish:** to put an end to a system, practice, or institution. *(Ezekiel 6:6; Ephesians 2:15; Esther 8:9; 1 Corinthians 15:24)*

**Accomplish:** achieve or complete successfully. *(John 4:34; Job 15:32; 2 Corinthians 8:11; Job 37:12; Philippians 2:13)*

**Accusation:** a charge or claim that someone has done something illegal or wrong. *(Exodus 23:1; Deuteronomy 19:16; Revelation 12:10)*

**Advance:** move forward in a purposeful way. (Joshua 6:5, 7; 8:5; Psalm 18:29; Jeremiah 46:3).

**Advantage:** the opportunity to gain something; to benefit or profit.

**Affliction:** something that causes pain or suffering. *(Genesis 41:52; Exodus 3:7; Job 30:16; Psalm 25:18; 91:10; Mark 5:34; Romans 5:3; 2 Corinthians 4:17)*

**Agree:** to have the same opinion about something; concur. *(Amos 3:3; Matthew 18:19; Acts 15:15; 1 Corinthians 1:10; 1 John 5:8)*

**Agreement:** harmony or accordance in opinion or feeling; a position or result of agreeing; the absence of incompatibility between two things; consistency. *(Genesis 9:9, 12; Exodus 6:5)*

**Alignment:** a position of agreement or alliance. *(Psalm 119:133; Proverbs 16:3)*

**Ancient Doors:** doors that have been closed for a long time. David declared, "Open up, you ancient gates, and the King of glory will come in" *(Psalm 24:7).*

**Annihilate:** to cause to cease to exist: to do away with entirely so that nothing remains; to destroy a considerable part of (*Genesis 6:13; Exodus 23:23; 2 Samuel 22:41; Psalm 92:7*).

**Anniversary Spirit:** the annual recurrence of a date marking a notable event.

**Anxiety:** a feeling of fear, dread, and uneasiness. *(1 Chronicles 21:13; Ecclesiastes 11:10; Luke 12:29)*

**Anxious:** experiencing worry, unease, or nervousness, typically about an imminent event or something with an uncertain outcome. *(Philippians 4:6)*

**Arrest:** to bring to a stop; to make inactive. *(Numbers 25:4; 1 Kings 18:40; Acts 9:14)*

**Arrow:** an injurious weapon that has the capacity to cause damage or death to an individual. *(Psalm 76:3; 144:6; Zechariah 9:14)*

**Arrows of Affliction:** arrows fired resulting in various ailments and oppression. Such sickness most times defies medication. *(Acts 15:36-41)*

**Arrow of Confusion:** causes friction in marriages, ministries, and organizations; separates friends. *(Acts 15:36-41)*

**Arrow of Darkness:** any arrow fired from the shrine or evil altar to cause commotion in our homes and/or family members.

**Arrow of Death:** untimely death, most of which comes suddenly. *(2 Kings 4:18-22; Mark 5:35)*

**Arrow of Deliverance:** an act of declaring war on one's enemies. There was an ancient custom to shoot an arrow or cast a spear into the country that an army intended to invade. *(2 Kings 13:19)*

**Arrow of Destiny Manipulation:** arranged to alter the divine course of life;

36

will make one experience terrible failures and setbacks in various aspects of life.

**Arrow of Devouring:** sent to attack one's wealth and properties. It can come because of sudden mishap resulting in great losses, or a collapse of business with great shortage.

**Arrow of Division:** causes division, including divorce in marriage. *(Acts 15:30 -41)*

**Arrows of Fire:** These weapons can be offensive and defensive by shooting flaming arrows. *(Psalm 76:3; Ephesians 6:16)*.

**Arrow of Generational Strongholds and Curses:** known for causing a cycle of evil within a family, it can be a particular kind of sickness or disease that is common within a family, or people dying young within a family, delays in marriage or childbearing, or difficulty in having breakthroughs within the family. It may be because of a curse pronounced upon the family or the generation at a particular time.

**Arrow (Gladiator):** that which does not manifest instantly but goes step by step to destroy its victim gradually and silently.

**Arrow of Rejection:** causes one to feel inadequate, insufficient, or not good enough. *(Job 8:20; Psalm 27:9; Romans 11:15)*

**Ascend:** to rise from a lower level or degree. *(Psalm 24:3; 122:4; 132:8; 139:8; Obadiah 21)*

**Atmosphere:** the pervading tone or mood of a place, situation, or work of art. *(Exodus 20:11; 1 Corinthians 14:9-10; 2 Corinthians 12:2)*

**Authority:** the power or right to give orders, make decisions, and enforce obedience; the power or ability to do something given by, conferred upon, or derived from a higher authority. It is the warrant, right, power, or ability to do something. *(Matthew 28:18; Luke 10:19; John 19:11; Romans 13:1)*

**Authorize:** to endorse, empower, justify, or permit by or as if by some recognized or proper authority such as custom, evidence, personal right, or regulating power; a custom authorized by time; to invest, especially with legal authority: empower. *(Nehemiah 2:7-10; 1 Corinthians 16:3; Revelation 11:3)*

**Awake(n):** cause to stop sleeping. *(Genesis 28:16; Judges 5:12; Psalm 3:5; Mark 14:37; John 11:11; Romans 13:11; Acts 12:7)*

**Awakening:** an act or moment of becoming suddenly aware of something. *(Acts 16:27)*

**Axe to the root:** there's a much deeper work than merely cutting off the branches and leaves. Christ came to deal with the root of the problem. He goes past the surface and deals with issues that lie hidden beneath what generally meets the eye. *(Matthew 3:10)*

# *Prayer Point*

*May the Blood of Jesus, arise and shatter to desolation all networking and trafficking witchcraft, wicked and evil workings in the heavens, firmament, air, land, and sea in the name of the Lord Jesus.*

*—Apostle James Phred Kawalya*
*Lifeway Church of Christ*
*Kampala, Uganda*

# B

**Backfire:** of a plan or action; return to the originator, often with negative consequences. *(Isaiah 55:8-11; Romans 11:9)*

**Barricade:** a barrier erected across a street or other thoroughfare to prevent or delay the movement of opposing forces: obstacles. *(Ezekiel 3:24; Luke 19:43)*

**Be Disgraced:** to be humiliated and brought to shame. *(Numbers 12:14; Psalm 25:2-3; 40:14-15; Isaia 45:16; Colossians 2:15)*

**Bind:** to make secure by tying; to confine, restrain, or restrict as if with bonds; to constrain legal authority; to form a firm commitment for; to have an emotional attachment; to hinder free operation. In refence to bind and loosing, it is originally a Jewish Mishnaic phrase mentioned in the New Testament. To properly use bind and loose means to forbid by an indisputable authority and to permit by an indisputable authority. Isaiah gives an example of how fasting can loosen the chains of injustice. *(Isaiah 58:5-6; Matthew 18:18-20; Acts 2:14-40)*

**Blind:** obstruction to sight or discernment. *(Genesis 48:8; 2 Kings 6:17; Isaiah 35:5; 2 Corinthians 4:6)*

**Blockage:** an object or structure that stops something from passing through. *(Isaiah 57:14; Ezekiel 34:25; 1 Thessalonians 2:18)*

**Blood of Jesus/Blood Block:** the blood of Jesus creates a border—a wall against the enemy. *(Psalm 121:7-8; Proverbs 18:10)*

**Boa Constrictor:** The name "boa" covers a whole family of snakes—more than fifty (50) species. Inside, they have tiny bones where a lizard's legs would start. Most boas give birth to live babies—they don't lay eggs. Boas don't chase their prey. They are ambush predators. Boas hide and remain still until prey comes close. Then, they strike quickly to catch it. Once it has prey in its teeth, a

Terri J. Davis

boa quickly wraps itself around the animal or person. It squeezes so tightly that the animal's lungs cannot expand, and its heart stops. Then, the boa swallows its prey whole, usually headfirst. Digestion takes a long time because food isn't in smaller chunks. The image of a spiritual boa constrictor wrapped around a person could symbolize that the spiritual life is being squeezed out through deception or forms of wickedness. *(Isaiah 1:18-25)*

**Bow down:** an action that shows one's respect for another, which is also a sign of agreement that the person is more powerful than one. *(2 Chronicles 29:29)*

**Break:** to separate into parts with suddenness or violence. *(Exodus 34:13; Leviticus 26:13; Job 28:4; Ezekiel 30:22)*

**Break forth:** to burst out forcefully suddenly; emerge. *(2 Samuel 23:16; 1 Chronicles 14:11; Proverbs 3:10; Micah 2:13)*

**Breakthrough:** a sudden, dramatic, and important discovery or development. *(2 Samuel 5:20-21; 2 Kings 7:6; Micah 2:13)*

**Broken Heart:** a state of extreme grief or sorrow, typically caused by the death of a loved one or the ending of a romantic relationship. *(Psalm 30:2; 34:18; 147:3)*

**Broken Hedge:** when confusion or sickness invades the camp (ministry or minister of the Gospel) of assigned intercessors, the wall is broken—which allows the enemy to launch an open attack through the practice of high-level witchcraft. This also causes spiritual weight, power, and influence to be sifted by the enemy. This is a demonic military strategy of surrounding the camp (ministry or minister) for the purpose of dismantling and destruction.

**Burden of Prayer:** "A prayer burden is a spiritual concern on the heart of God that is imparted by the Holy Spirit to someone whose intercession the Holy Spirit desires to use.... It is a specially sacred level of prayer intensity and prayer responsibility."—*Wesley Duewel*

**Burn by Fire:** Ask the Lord to release His fire and burn up the works of darkness. *(Genesis 19:24; 1 Kings 18:24; Psalm 104:4)*

# *Prayer Point*

*Precious Jesus, I thank you for peace that surpasses all my understanding. I will allow that peace to lead me as I journey through life, for I know you are with me. I am not afraid, I stand in the strength of Your word, knowing You will guide me. Blessed be the name of the Lord who causes me to triumph over my enemies. In the name of the Lord Jesus. Amen.*

# C

**Cancel:** to decide or announce that a planned event will not take place. *(Deuteronomy 15:1-2; Isaiah 28:18; 43:25; Colossians 2:14)*

**Capacity:** the maximum amount that something can contain or produce; the ability or power to do, experience, or understand something; a specified role or position. *(Genesis 44:1; Ezra 7:21; Mark 4:33)*

**Captivity:** the state of a person who has been taken prisoner. *(Deuteronomy 21:10; 30:3; Ezra 6:21; Psalm 53:6; Isaiah 52:2; Philippians 1:7, 14, 16)*

**Chain:** fasten or secure with a chain. *(Psalm 73:6; Isaiah 51:14; Luke 8:29)*

**Circumcision:** the cutting of the foreskin of males that is practiced as a religious rite. It is also a social custom for potential health benefits, such as improved hygiene. The circumcision of the heart is a radical change, an inner transformation, whereby in faith we receive humility, faith, hope, and love. Scripture passage for the sermon: "Circumcision is that of the heart, in the spirit and not in the letter." *(Genesis 17:10-14; Romans 2:29)*

**Collapse:** to fall or cave in; give way. *(Numbers 14:9; Joshua 6:15-20; Jeremiah 13:18)*

**Collective Captivity:** to be locked inside a demonic prison. Persons lose everything and are unable to move forward in life; the urge to give up is overwhelming, and they are slaves to the demonic. This captivity is a form of bondage that affects the individual and his or her family members. It functions as a kind of generational curse. People experience the consequences of actions that they did not commit. There are four types of captivity: (1) *Internal Captivity*—a type of confinement by a local force; the spirit of sabotage works against efforts to achieve success; (2) *External Captivity*—to be in the custody of an external force; (3) *Remote Control Captivity*—occurs when an evil spirit dominates the life of a person who, while under the influence of an evil force, discovers that they do things against his or her will; (4) *Personal Captivity*—occurs when one is not at peace within, thus being held captive by his or her thoughts. *(Exodus 1; Acts 1–17)*

**Compassion:** the capacity to be *caring and full of mercy. (Psalm 103:8; 145:8-9; Lamentations 3:22; Luke 6:36; 2 Corinthians 1:3)*

**Conceal:** to keep something a secret, prevent it from being known or noticed. *(Genesis 37:26; 1 Samuel 3:18; 19:2; Proverbs 25:2)*

**Conquer:** overcome and take control of a place or people by use of military force; to successfully overcome a problem or weakness. *(Numbers 22:6; Judges 1:19; Psalm 60:12; Obadiah 17; Romans 8:37; 12:21)*

**Consecration:** the act of making or declaring something as sacred or set apart to the service of God; devotion to a purpose in a very sincere manner. *(Exodus 28:3; 29:33; 2 Chronicles 29:17)*

**Covenant:** a legally binding agreement which brings about a relationship of commitment between God and His people. The word *covenant* derives from the same root word meaning "to cut." This means that in the culture of the Bible, a covenant carried weight and was often cut, or sealed, in blood. *(Genesis 6:18; 9:9-17; Deuteronomy 4:13; Psalm 89:3; Matthew 26:28)*

**Crippled:** to be disabled or deficient in a specified manner; deprived of capability for service or of strength, efficiency, or wholeness. *(2 Samuel 4:4; Luke 13:11; Acts 3:2)*

# *Prayer Point*

*I overcome my accuser by the blood of Jesus and the word of my testimony which is the word of God, and I lay my life down as a living sacrifice unto the Lord. In the name of the Lord Jesus. Amen.*

# D

**Dance:** a series of movements that match the speed and rhythm of a piece of music. *(Psalm 149:3; 150:4; Ecclesiastes 3:4; Jeremiah 31:4; Luke 6:23)*

**Dawning:** the approaching of the morning light; the breaking of the day; a new start. *(Genesis 19:15; 32:22-26; Luke 1:78-79)*

**Declare:** to proclaim or announce officially or publicly. *(Exodus 7:1-2; Leviticus 23:4; Deuteronomy 15:1; Psalm 147:19; Isaiah 14:22)*

**Decree:** an official order issued by a legal authority. *(Numbers 10:8; 18:8: 31:21; Deuteronomy 28:8; Ezra 7:21; Job 22:28; Psalm 148:6)*

**Defeat:** win a victory over someone or something in a battle or another contest; overcome or beat. *(Deuteronomy 7:2; Joshua 11:8; Judges 6:16; 2 Kings 3:18-19; Zechariah 10:5)*

**Defend:** to guard against an attack; to speak or write in favor of an action or person; to conduct the case for the party being accused. *(1 Kings 8:45; 2 Kings 19:34; Job 13:6; Psalm 10:18; 72:4; Isaiah 31:5; Philippians 1:7)*

**Defense:** the act of protecting someone or something against an attack. *(2 Kings 11:6; Psalm 62:6; Isaiah 25:4; Jude 3)*

**Deliver:** to bring and hand over a letter, parcel, or ordered goods to the proper recipient or address; to set free; to give up or over, draw out. *(Genesis 32:11; Psalm 25:20; 70:5; 143:9; Jeremiah 7:10; Ezekiel 3:19)*

**Demolish:** to pull or knock down a building; to refute an argument or its proponent; to overthrow, tear down, or destroy. *(2 Corinthians 10:5)*

**Demon:** an angelic being who rebelled with Satan and was expelled from heaven. Demons are also called "the knowing ones." Demons know information based upon information from the spirit realm and observation. *(Matthew 4:10; 8:16; Mark 1:34; Luke 4:41; 11:14)*

**Demonic Cage:** an enclosure (such as a box or coffin) made with metal wires or a net. It is specifically made for the purpose of trapping and confining, an arena of limitation, bondage, and lack of freedom. A spiritual circle has been drawn around an individual or family. *(Isaiah 49:24; Jeremiah 5:25-26)*

**Demonic Contract:** One enters into a formal and legally binding agreement with a demon by blood covenant. One's having a debt that he or she cannot influence, or control is far more a liability than ever imagined. *(Proverbs 17:18)*

**Demonic Influence:** Possession, in which Satan or demons take full possession of a person's body without his or her consent. *(Mark 5:1-20; 1 Corinthians 10:21)*

**Demonic Intelligence:** This ability of evil spirits to speak is evident in the four gospels and in the book of Acts. A study of the Scriptures makes it clear that demon spirits are intelligent: they can possess specific information about things, places, or people; They can know the names of people; They can indwell a human being and engage that person's vocal apparatus to terrorize others, to blaspheme, to challenge, to make requests, and to scream, shriek, and cry out. *(Matthew 8:29; Mark 5:7-12; Acts 19:15)*

**Demonic Network:** The kingdom of darkness is highly organized and operates strategically. Satan uses demonic technology against us based on information that has been diligently researched. The enemy's demonic agents—such as familiar spirits, monitoring demons, drones, satanic surveillances, and other intel systems—gather information about us, our families, our strengths and weaknesses, and so forth; and with such data, they seek to devise a cleverly constructed system through which to destroy us. *(Ephesians 6:12)*

**Demonic Power:** Demons have power, but through the working of the Holy

Terri J. Davis

Spirit, we can resist and overcome their power. *(Luke 10:19)*

**Denounce:** to publicly state that someone or something is bad or wrong. *(Numbers 23:8; 1 Samuel 2:23-24; Titus 1:13; 1 Peter 3:16)*

**Deploy:** to move troops or equipment into position for military action; to bring into effective action; to move, spread out, or place in position for some purpose. *(Psalm 27:3; Jeremiah 46:3; 2 Samuel 10:17; Nahum 2:3)*

**Despair:** the complete loss or absence of hope. *(Job 6:14; Psalm 61:2; Proverbs 14:10; Jeremiah 5:19)*

**Destroy:** to put an end to the existence of something by damaging or attacking it; to defeat someone utterly. *(Exodus 34:13; Deuteronomy 4:31; 7:2; Isaiah 10:27)*

**Dethrone:** to remove from a position of authority or dominance. *(Haggai 2:22)*

**Diabolical:** relating to or proceeding from the devil; satanic; befitting a devil; extremely cruel or wicked; fiendish.

**Dilute:** to make a liquid thinner or weaker by adding water or another solvent to it.

**Dimension:** a measurement of something in a particular direction, especially its height, length, or width. *(Ephesians 3:18-19)*

**Disallow:** to refuse to allow; reject; veto. *(1 Corinthians 13:6; 1 Thessalonians 5:22)*

**Disarm:** to take a weapon or weapons away from a person, force, or country. *(Isaiah 45:1; Colossians 2:15)*

**Disbelief:** the inability or refusal to believe or to accept something as true. *(Romans 3:3; Hebrews 4:6)*

46

**Discern:** to recognize the true worth or validity of something; to examine, prove, or test; scrutinize. *(1 Kings 3:9; Luke 12:54-56; Hebrews 5:14)*

**Discernment:** supernatural insight; the ability to choose between what is true and right and what is false and wrong; distinguishing; it is a "knowing" that can feel like a gut instinct—but it does not originate with us. True discernment is born out of intimacy with the Father, praying in the Spirit and surrendering our five senses to the Holy Spirit. *(Philippians 1:9-10; 1 Thessalonians 5:21-22; 2 Timothy 2:7; Hebrews 5:14)*

**Discord:** a state of distrust among people, which results in arguments and fights done in secret. *(Proverbs 6:12-14)*

**Discouragement:** a loss of confidence or enthusiasm; dispiritedness; a temptation "common to man" in dealing with it; sometimes we need tenderness and other times we need toughness. It develops when the comparing mind holds unrealistic expectations, demands perfection, and craves measurable progress, predictable results, or signposts of success. *(Joshua 1:9; 1 Corinthians 10:13)*

**Dismantle:** to take something (such as a machine or structure) apart so that it is in separate pieces. *(Ezekiel 30:4)*

**Distraction:** a thing that prevents us from giving full attention to something else. *(1 Corinthians 7:35; Colossians 3:2)*

**Divine Intelligence:** the omniscient (all-knowing) God who has infinite knowledge; also, the latent, unlimited potential in human beings. *(Psalm 139:6)*

**Divine Settlement:** supernatural restoration to a place of glory, power, peace, and rest. It can be in the form of restored health, deliverance, a good job, fruit of the womb, a husband or wife, marital peace, a good home, or restoration. It means "a favorable turnaround of a matter." *(Exodus 3:7-8; Job 42:10-16; 1 Peter 5:10)*

**Divine Timing:** the belief that everything that happens in our lives occurs at precisely the right moment. *(Ecclesiastes 3:1; Isaiah 43:19)*

**Dominion:** the territory of a sovereign or government. *(Genesis 1:16, 26-28)*

**Doubt:** a feeling of uncertainty about; consider questionable or unlikely; hesitate to believe. *(Psalm 50:15; Isaiah 41:13; James 1:5-8; I John 5:14)*

**Dry Places:** spaces that are *spiritually* dry—that is, places where God is absent. *(Matthew 12:43)*

**Dynamic:** a force that stimulates change or progress within a system or process. *(James 5:16)*

# *Prayer Point*

*Father, help and heal my unbelief. I cast my fears and cares upon you for I know that you will tend to them. Thank you for the spirit of overcoming fear and the courage to believe in the mighty name of Jesus. Amen.*

# E

**Emotional Wrecker:** one who causes emotional distress—such as confusion, heartbreak, anger, and sadness—by way of dishonest behavior.

**Encountering God:** to be welcomed into His all-consuming presence; this is where we learn our identity in Christ. *(Genesis 18:1-10; 32–33; Exodus 33:17-23)*

**Enemy Camp:** a place suitable for or used as a temporary place of rest. *(Judges 7:13-25; 1 Samuel 29–30)*

**Enforce:** to cause something to happen by necessity or force. *(Psalm 106:2; Jeremiah 20:11; Ezekiel 44:24)*

**Eradicate:** to destroy completely; put an end to. *(Ecclesiastes 3:2; Daniel 7:26)*

**Establish:** to install or settle in a position, place, business, etc. *(Genesis 17:2; 2 Samuel 7:13; 1 Chronicles 16:15; 2 Thessalonians 3:3)*

**Evil Altars:** places where many evil things are projected into people's lives, such as infirmities, curses, and failures—among other things. These altars are placed *in rooms of Powers (Ephesians 6:12) of enchanters and diviners. Here is where the wicked consult* their gods. *(Psalm 27:12-13; Daniel 7:23; Matthew 5:25; Romans 12:2; 1 Corinthians 6:2-3; 1 John 2:1-2; Revelation 12:10)*

**Excavate:** to extract material from the ground by digging. *(Genesis 26:15-32)*

**Expel:** to force out or eject something, especially from the body. *(Deuteronomy 7:22; Matthew 8:31; 10:8; 12:28)*

Terri J. Davis

**Expose:** to make something visible by uncovering it. *(Isaiah 3:17; Ephesians 5:11)*

**Expunge:** to erase or remove completely something unwanted or unpleasant.

**Extinguish:** to put an end to an event, situation. *(2 Samuel 21:17; Song of Solomon 8:7; Isaiah 42:3; Matthew 12:20; Ephesians 6:16)*

*Thank you, Holy Ghost, that you are for us and on our side in every area. I thank You Lord because will not withhold any good thing from those who love You and are called according to Your purpose. Father, thank you for initiating this love for there is no spirit of pride, no spirit of arrogance, no spirit of embarrassment Father, we need You for You are the source of our life and the source of our strength. Father, right now in the name of Jesus, cast out and curse every spirit especially the spirit of poverty that has come against your people. Every generational curse, every generational mindset associated with poverty I break it now in the name of Jesus. I break and bind every religious spirit associated with poverty. I break the spirit of lack of discipline. I pray that their seed will bare good fruit in its time. You are the sustainer of life and the keeper of our wealth and resources. I speak to the worry and pressure that is making you sick. Every health defect, every spirit of infirmity attacking your body through the spirit of poverty, I cast it out in the name of the Lord Jesus Christ the Redeemer. God has a simple financial plan for the Believer, tithes and offering and I speak to multiplication in your life in Jesus' name. Amen.*

*—Apostle DaVaughn L. Williams*
*Christ Embassy Tennessee*

# F

**Faith:** belief and trust in and loyalty to God; firm belief, even in the absence of proof. *(Acts 26:18; Ephesians 2:8-9; Hebrews 3:6)*

**Faith, (Dead):** one who is lacking good fruit and has an abundance of selfish thoughts, cruel words, and immoral deeds. Faith without works is dead. *(James 2:17)*

**Faith, (Demonic):** Their "faith" is intellectual—that is, the demons have no doubt that Jesus is the Son of the living God, but they rebelliously choose to serve a different master; even demons believe and shudder at the name of Jesus. *(James 2:19)*

**Faith, (Saving):** God loves every one of us so much that He sent His only begotten Son to live among us—and whoever believes on Jesus will have eternal life. We are saved by grace through faith. Salvation is a gift. *(John 3:16; Romans 10:9-10; Ephesians 2:8-10)*

**Faithful:** being steadfast in affection or allegiance; loyal: a faithful friend, firm in adherence to promises or in observance of duty; conscientious: a faithful employee. *(Exodus 34:7; Deuteronomy 7:9; 1 Samuel 3:20; 2 Samuel 22:31; Psalm 145:13; 146:6; Matthew 25:21-25; 1 Corinthians 4:2; Hebrews 3:6)*

**Faithless:** one who is not loyal and not able to be trusted; lacks confidence in God's Word. *(Luke 8:25)*

**Father:** a male parent; a man who has begotten a child(ren). *(Genesis 17:4-7; Mark 14:36)*

**Father of Lights:** God is the Father of Lights, or "of heavenly lights." He *is* the source of the light. *(James 1:17)*

**Fear:** a feeling of anxiety concerning the outcome of something or the safety and well-being of someone. *(Psalm 34:4; Proverbs 29:25; Isaiah 41:10; 2 Timothy 1:7)*

**Fear of the Lord:** "The fear of the LORD is the beginning of knowledge." Until we understand who God is and develop a reverential fear of Him, we cannot have true wisdom. True wisdom comes only from understanding who God is and that He is holy, just, and righteous but He hates sin. *(Proverbs 1:7)*

**Fiery Darts:** things that manifest as fear, impure thoughts, or hatred; "flaming arrows" (NIV). *(Proverbs 26:18-19; Ephesians 6:16)*

**Fight:** to take part in a violent struggle involving the exchange of physical blows or the use of weapons; to engage in a war or battle. *(Exodus 14:14; Psalm 43:1; 119:154; Ephesians 6:12)*

**Finished:** brought a task or activity to an end; completed; performed; carried out; fulfilled. *(Genesis 49:33; Exodus 31:18; Psalm 18:37; John 19:30)*

**Fire on the Altar:** believers' hearts constitute the altar, and fire is the presence of God. *(Leviticus 6:12-13)*

**Floodgates:** gates that can be opened or closed to admit or exclude water, especially the lower gates of a lock; a last restraint holding back an outpouring of something powerful or substantial. *(Genesis 8:2; Malachi 3:10)*

**Forgive:** to cease to feel resentment against an offender; to give up resentment of or claim to requital. *(2 Chronicles 7:14)*

**Forgiven:** having (been) pardoned (an offender). *(Numbers 14:19; Luke 7:48)*

**Forgiveness:** the act of letting go of sin or guilt; forgiving everyone, every time, of everything, as an act of obedience and gratefulness to God. *(Leviticus 5:13; Numbers 14:19; Psalm 25:11)*

**For His Name's Sake:** God is acting in accordance with His revealed character—H*is integrity, reputation, holiness;* to uphold the honor of His revelation, which has been staked upon His people. The name of the Lord approves His plan. *(Psalm 23; Acts 4:1-22)*

**Fortify:** to build up a place with defensive works as protection against attack. *(Psalm 51:18)*

**Fowl of the Air:** natural birds (as it also stands for demons, the spirit of death, rumor spreaders, and demonic messengers). *(Psalm 91:3; Ecclesiastes 10:20)*

**Freemasonry:** the teachings and practices of the fraternal order of Free and Accepted Masons, the largest worldwide secret society. These individuals take an oath as part of the initiation process. *(Matthew 5:34)*

**Fresh Oil:** a new anointing poured out by God. All things become new. *(Psalm 92:10)*

**Friendly Fire:** weapon fire coming from one's own side, especially fire that causes accidental injury or death to one's own forces.

# *Prayer Point*

*Through the blood of Jesus, I renounce, untangle, and destroy all ancestral spirits of freemasonry, Shriners, idolatry, fraternity, sorority, witchcraft, false religion, polygamy, lust, and perversion. I am a joint heir with Jesus Christ; therefore, I am counted as a son. I am no longer held captive by sins of my ancestors. I stand as them asking for repentance for the sin of idolatry. May the blood of Jesus cleanse my bloodline and remove all residue of the sin in the name of Jesus. Amen.*

# G

**Garment of Praise:** God gives us a garment of praise instead of a spirit of despair. *(Isaiah 61:3)*

**Gates:** hinged barriers used to close openings in walls, fences, or hedges. *(Genesis 24:60; 2 Chronicles 23:19; Psalm 9:14; 24:7-9)*

**Gates of Brass:** obstructions, hindrances, and roadblocks. Everything that obstructs and hinders us from moving forward and making progress in life. *(Deuteronomy 33:25; Isaiah 45:2)*

**Gates of Bronze:** the things that have held us back for years. Addictions, lack, depression, and insecurity may have been in our families for generations. God is putting an end to it. *(Deuteronomy 33:25; Psalm 107:16; Isaiah 45:2)*

**Gates of Hell (Hades):** entryways to hell. *(Matthew 16:17-19)*

**Gates of Iron:** these things confront both the believer and the unbeliever—but God provides safe passage through them if we turn to Him. *(Deuteronomy 33:25; Psalm 107:16; Isaiah 45:2; Acts 12:10)*

**Gates, (Possess the):** whoever possesses the gates controls the dynamics of a region. That control can bring in a move of God or it can shut down the heavens—depending on who possesses the gates. *(Genesis 24:60)*

**Gates, (Secure the):** when a group of intercessors comes together in covenant prayer for a series of days and a set time, to pray for a particular situation regarding a person, place, or thing. This requires the group to maintain integrity with one another, time, repentance, worship, and warfare. They will secure the gates of the spirit realm that will hinder the work of witchcraft for an expanded period of years. *(Genesis 24:60)*

**Generational Blessings:** the continued covering of God's covenant over our families from generation to generation. *(Genesis 12:1-3)*

**Generational Curses:** misfortunes that tend to happen repeatedly—from one generation to the next—caused by sin, disobedience, or witchcraft. *(Exodus 34:7; Romans 5:19; 11:11-24)*

**Get to the Root:** to figure out the essential part or cause of something. *(Job 19:28)*

**Gift of Administration:** the ability to maintain order and be in agreement with God's principles and people. *(Romans 12:8; 1 Corinthians 12:28)*

**Gift of Discerning Spirits:** the ability to recognize whether something is truly from God or in accordance with His righteousness. The ability to detect motivation and the spirits that motivate; the ability to aid the church, set people free, protect the integrity of what God is doing, and help us overcome in spiritual warfare. *(Matthew 10:16; 1 Corinthians 12:10)*

**Gift of Faith:** the ability to trust God and inspire others to trust God, no matter the conditions. The Lord has empowered us to move to new levels of faith to do miracles and wonders in His name. *(1 Corinthians 12:9)*

**Gift of Healing:** the wondrous gift of using God's healing power to cure persons who are ill, wounded, or suffering. *(1 Corinthians 14:1)*

**Gift of Helps:** the desire and capacity to always help others achieve a task. *(1 Corinthians 12:28)*

**Gift of Interpreting:** the ability to interpret the speech and writing of a different language and translate it back to others in their own understanding. *(1 Corinthians 14:28)*

Terri J. Davis

**Gift of Knowledge:** the ability to comprehensively understand a spiritual issue or circumstance and know something that you cannot be known based on human intelligence. *(1 Corinthians 12:8)*

**Gift of Miracles:** the ability to display miracles, signs, and wonders that give credibility to God's Word and the Gospel message. This spiritual gift is manifested by the Holy Spirit, not human efforts. The work is unexplainable by nature. It edifies and delivers others. *(1 Corinthians 12:10)*

**Gift of Prophecy:** the gift to declare a message and understand the mysteries of God to edify and build them up. *(1 Corinthians 14:4, 24-25)*

**Gift of Tongues:** one's ability to communicate in a foreign language with which he or she has no experience; to converse with those who speak that language; a supernatural ability to speak and pray in an unknown tongue. *(1 Corinthians 12:10; 14:21-22)*

**Gift of Wisdom:** works with the word of knowledge. It gives one the ability and understanding of how to apply the word of knowledge. It allows a person to understand things from God's point of view. *(Proverbs 2:6; 1 Corinthians 12:8; James 3:17)*

**Gifts of the Spirit:** it is God's empowering faithful His people to do what He has called us to do. The gifts of the Holy Spirit provide everything we need to accomplish His plans. All gifts of the Spirit require love—love of God and others. *(Romans 12:3-8; 1 Corinthians 12:8-10; Ephesians 4:7-13)*

**Glory:** a term used to describe the manifestation of God's presence; praise, honor, or distinction extended by common consent: renown; worshipful praise, honor, and thanksgiving; giving glory to God. *(Exodus 33:18; Proverbs 20:29; Isaiah 6:3; Matthew 4:8-10; John 8:49)*

**Grace:** the freely given, unmerited favor and love of God. *(Numbers 6:24-26; Psalm 103:8; 2 Corinthians 8:9; Hebrews 4:16; 1 Peter 5:10)*

**Grip of Death:** an extremely tight grip caused especially by fear. *(Job 9:34; Psalm 116:3; Romans 5:17)*

**Guerrilla Warfare:** a small, loosely organized army that fights a larger, stronger force. If you are a guerrilla, you confront enemies unexpectedly and use tactics such as sabotage, raids, and ambushes. This type of warfare is structured to attack our mental health, finances, relationships, career, and family. *(Micah 7:6, Matthew 10:36; Ephesians 6:10-13)*

**Guilt:** a feeling of deserving blame for offenses. *(Isaiah 1:18; Romans 8:1; 1 John 1:9)*

# *Prayer Point*

*Father, I honor You. For You are gracious and full of compassion; slow to anger, and of great mercy (Ps. 145:8). Your great compassion and love for Your children was displayed on a rugged cross where Your only begotten Son, Jesus, gave His life for the sins of the world. Without Your love, we would be lost sheep wandering in a pasture with no direction. I pray that we become sensitive to Your voice and move with discernment. Father, continue to endow Your servants with discernment and intelligence and cause us to be skillful in all wisdom so that we will be competent to stand in the presence of a king and serve in his palace (Dan. 1:4). Father God, this great compassion You give to us is new every morning; so, I say thank You and I love You. It is in Your Son Jesus' name, Amen.*

*—Psalmist Davena Witherspoon*
*Lebanon, TN*

# H

**Hard Heart:** possessed by a person lacking sympathetic understanding; a heart that is stubborn or unrepentant. *(Ezekiel 36:26; Romans 2:5; Hebrews 3:8, 13)*

**Heal:** treatment of a wound, injury, or person; to become sound or healthy again; restore; cure; make well. *(2 Kings 20:8; 2 Chronicles 7:14; Psalm 103:3; Hosea 6:2; Matthew 8:7; Luke 9:1; James 5:15)*

**Healing:** the process of making or becoming sound or healthy again; alleviating a person's distress or anguish. *(Exodus 15:26; Psalm 103:3; Proverbs 4:22; 12:18; Matthew 9:35; Luke 9:11)*

**Hedge:** a supernatural, godly boundary to protect our faith, family, friends, decisions, principles, service, and church family. *(Ecclesiastes 10:8; Ezekiel 13:5)*

**Hinder:** to create difficulties for someone or something, resulting in delay or obstruction. *(Genesis 24:56; Galatians 5:7; 1 Thessalonians 2:18; 1 Peter 3:7)*

**Honey:** a sweet, viscid fluid produced by bees from the nectar collected from flowers and stored in nests or hives as food. This substance is used in cooking, as a spread, as a sweetener, or as medicine. *(Psalm 81:16; 119:103; Proverbs 16:24)*

**Honor:** high respect; great esteem; reverence. *(Leviticus 26:2; Joshua 4:14; 1 Chronicles 29:12)*

**Horns of the Wicked:** specialize in loss, shedding blood, and destroying lives and families. They are taskmasters, with a goal to scatter and demote. Corruption is what drives them. These wicked people work in concert with territorial, familiar, and generational spirits in our lives. *(Psalm 75:10; Zechariah 1:18-21)*

**Hunter:** one that searches for something; one trained to chase down something of interest. *(Genesis 10:9; 25:27)*

# *Prayer Point*

*Father, I prayer for the family structure that is under attack. Remind the husband and wife that they are to cling to one another. Teach them how to submit to one another and bring their marriage back to Your original intent and purpose. Cause their children to see them as godly role models. I take back the family and bring it under Your care by the blood of Jesus. It is by faith and Your word that I decree and declare that families and marriages will be healed and made whole in the name of the Lord Jesus. Amen.*

*—Pastor Donita L. Flippin*
*Ambassadors for Christ*
*Nashville, TN*

# I

**Ichabod:** a name meaning "Without glory"; "where is the glory?"; "the glory has departed." *(1 Samuel 4:21)*

**Immobilize:** to prevent something or someone from moving or operating as normal. *(Job 37:10)*

**Impede:** to delay or prevent (someone or something) by obstruction; hinder; hamper. *(Proverbs 4:12; 1 Corinthians 9:12)*

**Incantations:** a series of words spoken as a magic spell or charm. *(1 Chronicles 10:13)*

**Incapacitated:** prevented from functioning in a normal way. *(Leviticus 20:6; 1 Chronicles 10:13; Micah 5:12; Galatians 5:19-21)*

**Incubus:** male agents enchant women with sexual intercourse through the dream realm. This spirit approaches with a familiar face such as a former (or current) lover or a famous personality. This spirit causes uncontrollable masturbation urges and acts.

**Infiltrate:** (secretly) collect intelligence during a mission. *(2 Peter 2:1; Joshua 2)*

**Intelligence:** the ability to acquire and apply knowledge and skills. *(Jeremiah 3:15; Daniel 1:17; 5:12)*

**Intercession:** an act or instance of interceding; an interposing or pleading on behalf of another person. *(Genesis 18:16-33; Romans 8:26; 8:34; 1 Timothy 2:1)*

**Intercessor:** someone who prays, petitions, or begs God in favor of another person. *(Genesis 18:16-33; Isaiah 59:15-17; 1 Timothy 2:1)*

**Intercessors, (Types of):** Intercessors need to be well-versed and experienced in all types of intercession. Intercessors frequently find themselves interceding predominantly for one or two of these specific areas, but by no means does an intercessor always intercede in only one area.

**Intercessors, (Birthing or Midwife):** These intercessors love to "birth" souls, revivals, new ministries, schools, and godly businesses. This may involve travailing, which is a type of birthing intercession. Midwife intercessors sometimes help the travailing intercessor to give birth to what the Holy Spirit is wanting to birth.

**Intercessors, (Crisis) [Paramedics of Prayer]:** These intercessors rush in and out of the throne room with urgent requests on behalf of others—acting as watchmen for God's people. They are the ones He can wake up in the middle of the night to pray for someone they may or may not even know!

**Intercessors, (Financial):** those who have been anointed by God to summon funds on behalf of others.

**Intercessors, (Governmental):** the watchmen who prayerfully uphold the leaders in the church and political arenas where destinies are forged.

**Intercessors, (Issues):** These intercessors stand against injustices. The "issues" are what make them weep and pound the table!

**Intercessors, (List):** They find freedom in structure! As soon as they hear a prayer request, they look for a pen to document the request.

**Intercessors, (Mercy):** These intercessors are God's living stethoscopes. They can hear/feel the pain of others and want to extend the mercy of God to the root of that pain.

**Intercessors, (People—Group and Israel):** They are prayer shepherds for ethnic groups. God is calling intercessory shepherds to lead the way in prayer for entire people groups. Their hearts leap when they think of certain nations or ethnic groups, and they find themselves praying for those persons to be touched by God as a nation or group.

**Intercessors, (Personal):** Personal intercessors can be trusted with confidential information for which to pray for another person.

**Intercessors, (Prophetic):** These intercessors pray the things on God's heart; then, under His direction, they report the words, thoughts, images, and actions that He releases them to share (at His discretion). This level of intercession requires trust with the secrets of God. This is the highest-ranking order of an Intercessor.

**Intercessors, (Warfare):** These intercessors fight to usher in truth by establishing God's authority in places where the enemy has a "strong" hold on people, places, or situations.

**Intercessors, (Worship):** They access heaven's power (through worship) and bring hope to the hopeless. They silence the voice of the enemy and release the voice of the Beloved over people and situations; they are sacred romancers.

**Intimacy:** close familiarity or friendship; closeness; a private, cozy atmosphere; an intimate act. Intimacy with God requires obedience, prayer, sanctification, and the Word of God. *(Proverbs 19:22)*

**It's Not Over:** the outcome cannot be assumed or determined until given a solution.

# *Prayer Point*

*For every weak, vulnerable, bibleless person who put their hope in leaders more than their hope in God, may you turn from your idols you have made of man. May you turn your heart to God who is your hope and redeemer. In the name of Jesus, Amen.*

# J

**Joy:** a lasting emotion that comes from the choice to trust that God will fulfill His promises. *(Nehemiah 8:10; Proverbs 17:22; John 16:24; Romans 15:13; Galatians 5:22; James 1:2)*

**Judge:** one who is a public official appointed to decide cases in a court of law. It also carries the idea of having discernment. The Hebrew term, *Shofet,* refers to one who is a kind of military leader or deliverer. *(John 7:24)*

**Judgment:** the process whereby a verdict is reached, or the verdict itself. *(Matthew 12:36-37; John 5:21-25; 2 Corinthians 5:10; Hebrews 9:27-28; Revelation 20:12-15)*

**Jurisdiction:** the territory or sphere of activity over which the legal authority of a court or other institution extends. *(Matthew 9:8; John 5:27; Romans 9:21; 13:1-3; Titus 3:1)*

## *Prayer Point*

*Father every evil plan against my life, let them fall apart. Lord anything or device the enemy is using to track my progress, let them get destroyed by your fire. Crush every demonic activity of the enemy against my life. Arise oh Lord and destroy the plans of the enemies for my life. Lord do not allow evil to prevail over my life and family. Father, let the counsel of the wicked against my life backfire. Set my enemies against one another. Lord, deliver me from self-errors. Lord, place in me your glory would have a positive impact on my generation. I declare, what stopped my generation will not stop me in the name Jesus. Amen*

—*Pastor Blessing Olarewaju*

*Nigeria*

# K

**Kindness:** the quality of being friendly, generous, and considerate. *(1 Corinthians 13:4-7; Ephesians 4:32)*

**King:** a male ruler of a country who usually inherits his position and rules for life. *(Psalm 24:8-10)*

**Kingdom of Darkness:** It is the realm of demons, of Satan himself—who, according to the Bible, controls the earth's belief systems and seeks constantly to deceive and destroy mankind. It is a realm controlled by sin, death, and rebellion toward God. *(Romans 6:23; 2 Corinthians 4:4; Ephesians 2:1-6)*

**Kingdom of God:** *the rule of an eternal, sovereign God over all the universe—and Jesus is Lord.* the kingdom of God is not meat and drink, but righteousness, peace, and joy in the Holy Ghost. *(Luke 17:20-21; Romans 14:17)*

**Kingdom of Heaven:** the place where God resides and govern the universe. *(Matthew 13:24-54; 18:3)*

## *Prayer Point*

*Thank You Lord for forgiving my sins and washing me with Your word. I give myself to you daily for Your glory to be revealed in the earth. In Jesus name. Amen.*

# L

**Lament:** a way that we share our burdens, complaints, and confusion with God. He wants to hear from us. We must mentally lay our burdens at God's feet. *(Matthew 11:30; John 16:33)*

**Legal Grounds:** refers to a rational motive or basis for a belief, a conviction, or an action taken, such as a legal action or argument, reason, or cause. *(Exodus 20:5; Deuteronomy 7:26)*

**Legislate:** to perform the function of legislation; specifically, to make or enact laws. *(Matthew 6:10; 18:18; Hebrews 8:6)*

**Let God arise:** to be stirred up; to awake and prepare for action; when God arises on our behalf, all those who are against us, our families, business, and ministries will be in serious trouble. *(Numbers 10:35; Psalm 68:1-2)*

**Let my enemies be put to shame and disappointed:** David asked the Lord to put his enemies to shame and completely disappoint them. *(Psalm 35:4, 11-16)*

**Leviathan:** a sea serpent of tremendous strength, described as the most powerful and dangerous creature in the ocean; known as the King of Pride, a high-ranking principality. Only the Lord Himself can deal with Leviathan. *(Job 41; Psalm 74:14; 104:25-26)*

**Life:** the existence of an individual human being. *(Genesis 2:7; John 10:10)*

**Loose:** detached or able to be detached; to set free; release. *(Luke 13:10-17; John 8:36)*

**Love:** strong affection for another arising out of kinship or personal ties. *(John 3:16; 1 Corinthians 13:4-8)*

Terri J. Davis

**Lust:** a strong craving for sex or power. *(Psalm 81:12; Proverbs 6:25; Ezekiel 16:28-30; Matthew 5:28; Mark 7:21-22; 1 Corinthians 10:6)*

# *Prayer Point*

*Through the Blood of Jesus, I command all spirits of lust, perversion, adultery, fornication, uncleanliness, and immorality to come out of my life and my body in the name of the Lord Jesus.*

*—Apostle James Phred Kawalya*
*Lifeway Church of Christ*
*Kampala, Uganda*

# M

**"Make us more like You":** to have a desire to turn away from evil things and to become more like God—setting our hearts on His Word—and to pursue His heart. *(John 17:26)*

**Mantle:** The Hebrew word for "mantle" is addereth. It is glory, cloak, splendor, magnificence of a vine, shepherds made of fur or fine materials, a prophet's garment, robe. This garment is the authority that the prophet receives when he is ordained and set apart. A mantle is used to protect, but it also represents empowerment. *(1 Kings 19:13-19; 2 Kings 2:8-13)*

**Marine Kingdom:** This traces back to the demonic origins to the great flood of Noah. Creatures of this realm live in water and do not feel comfortable being dry. The Atlantic Ocean is governed by the Queen of the Sea, while the Indian Ocean is governed by the queen of the Coast. Both queens are Fallen Angels, and they are the lead cause of Marine influence upon the natural world. The Marine Spirit mostly operates in the dream realm, using sex as its initiating altar. Pride, beauty, and rebellion are also features/functions of these demons. These spirits are also connected to Chemosh, Ashtoreth, and Milcom (Molek). *(Genesis 1:28; 1 Kings 11:7, 33; Job 26:5; 38:8; Revelation 12:12)*

**Mercy:** forbearance and forgiveness shown, even though undeserved by the recipient *(Deuteronomy 4:31; Romans 9:15-16; Ephesians 2:4; 1 Peter 1:3)*

**Mermaid Spirit:** Mermaids are mythical sea creatures with the upper body of a female human and the tail of a fish. A mermaid's demeanor ranges from seductive to sinister. The person who submits to this spirit operates in witchcraft—such as chanting, psychic readings, horoscopes, white, yellow, or blue magic, etc., enticing another to be sexually involved, which creates a demonic covenant. *(2 Kings 9:22; Proverbs 6:25)*

**Might:** great or overwhelming power or strength. *(Ephesians 6:10)*

Terri J. Davis

**Miracle:** an extraordinary event taken as a sign of the supernatural power of God. *(Mark 1:30-31; Luke 5:1-11; John 2:1-11; John 4:46-47)*

# *Prayer Point*

*Every marine witchcraft spirit lodging in my family bloodline, be disgraced by fire, in the name of Jesus. I break the backbone of every marine witchcraft militating against my life with the hands of fire, in Jesus' name. Every work of marine witchcraft in my life, be destroyed by the blood of Jesus. I release my life from the grip of marine witchcraft, in the name of Jesus. Amen.*

# N

**Naked:** to be a person or part of the body that is without clothes; open to view; not concealed; manifest; destitute of worldly goods; exposed to shame and disgrace. *(Genesis 2:25; Exodus 32:25; Job 1:21; Hebrews 4:13)*

**Nakedness:** innocence, defenselessness, vulnerability, helplessness, humiliation, shame, guilt, or judgment; nudity; bareness. "Ye are spies; to see the *nakedness* of the land are ye come"; plainness; openness to view. *(Genesis 42:9; Deuteronomy 22:30; Ezekiel 22:10)*

**Neutralized:** counteracted the activity or effect of; made ineffective; fruitless. *(Ephesians 5:11)*

**New:** not existing before; made, introduced, or discovered recently or now for the first time. Unfamiliar, inexperienced, unaccustomed to doing something. *(Genesis 1:1; 2 Corinthians 5:17; Revelation 21:15)*

**Nightmare:** a terrifying dream in which the dreamer experiences feelings of helplessness, fear, extreme anxiety, or sorrow. Also known as a night terror. *(Psalm 91:5)*

**Nullify:** to cancel out; to make legally null and void; invalidate. *(Matthew 15:6; Romans 4:14; Galatians 3:17)*

# *Prayer Point*

*Love is patient and kind. Love is not jealous or boastful or proud or rude. It does not demand its own way. It is not irritable, and it keeps no record of being wronged. It does not rejoice about injustice but rejoices whenever the truth wins out. Love never gives up, never loses faith, is always hopeful, and endures through every circumstance. (I Corinthians 13:4-7) I eat the fruit of the Spirit, I become the fruit of the Spirit, and I display the attributes of the Fruit of the Spirit. In Jesus' name. Amen.*

# O

**Object of Affection:** a person in whom affection is centered or on whom one is dependent for affection or needed help. *(John 3:16; Ephesians 3:17-19; Romans 5:8)*

**Octopus:** a ruler (a master demonic spirit of darkness) of this world. Represent a controlling spirit due to the tentacles, witchcraft. Octopi can change the shape of their bodies and fit into the tiniest of places. The arms of the octopus are used to bring its prey to its mouth—where it will then be broken down with a sharp beak before being digested. There is a breaking down of a person that happens when he or she gives in to a sin of the flesh. The octopus spirit's main goal is to use whatever fleshly appetite a particular person is prone to give in to in a wrong or imbalanced way to bring that person into addictive, destructive, or obsessive patterns that he or she then becomes powerless to break free from without deliverance. *(Matthew 12:43-45)*

**Offend:** to cause hurt feelings or deep resentment. *(Psalm 25:3; 119:165; Isaiah 3:8)*

**Offense:** an act of attacking: assault. *(1 Samuel 25:28)*

**Oil of Joy:** a protective coating that shields people from offenses. *(Psalm 45:7)*

**Open Heaven:** a season of blessing when revelation is bountiful. *(Deuteronomy 28:1-14)*

**Open the Floodgates:** to make it possible for something to happen in great numbers. *(Genesis 7:11; 8:2)*

**Open the Understanding:** to be willing to consider new and different ideas or opinions. *(Ephesians 1:18)*

Terri J. Davis

**Open up:** to make something present, available, or accessible. *(Isaiah 41:18; 45:8; 2 Corinthians 6:13; Colossians 4:3)*

**Overthrow:** to remove forcibly from power. *(Deuteronomy 12:3; Proverbs 12:7; Amos 4:11; Haggai 2:22)*

**Overturn:** to tip something over so that it is on its side or upside down. *(Exodus 14:27; 34:13; Esther 8:3; Ezekiel 21:27; Haggai 2:22; Mark 13:2)*

**Oxidation of Armor:** When your spiritual armor has become worn out due to overexposure to oxygen, scientifically, silicon undergoes oxidation and forms silicon dioxide, which causes rust.

# *Prayer Point*

*Jehovah Gibbor, clothe Yourself in Your garments of war. Muster Your devices; gather Your weaponry and ammunition from Your divine arsenal. Make bright Your arrows, gather Your shields, and let vengeance be Your ultimate goal as You overthrow the chariots, horses, and riders. In Jesus' name. Amen.*

*—Dr. Cindy Trimm*
*Cindy Trimm Ministries International*
*Stockbridge, GA*

# P

**Pardon:** the action of forgiving or being forgiven for an error or offense. *(Exodus 34:9; Numbers 14:19; 2 Chronicles 7:14; Jeremiah 33:8; Matthew 6:15)*

**Peace:** freedom from disturbance; tranquility; a state or period in which there is no war or a war has ended. *(Isaiah 26:3; John 14:27; 16:33; 2 Thessalonians 3:16)*

**Persevere:** put forth continued effort to do or achieve something despite difficulties, failure, or opposition. *(Proverbs 4:25-26; Romans 5:3-5; 12:12; Galatians 6:9; Revelation 2:10)*

**Persistence:** firm or obstinate continuance in a course of action in spite of difficulty or opposition. *(Matthew 18:1-6)*

**Petition:** a request made for something desired, especially a respectful or humble request, to a superior or to one of those in authority. *(Philemon 6-7)*

**Pierce:** to make holes, especially decorated with perforations: having the flesh punctured. *(Judges 5:26; Job 41:2; Psalm 37:15; 45:5; John 19:34)*

**Plans:** a proposed or intended course of action. *(Jeremiah 29:11)*

**Plans of the Enemy:** to formulate a scheme or program for accomplishment, enactment, or attainment. *(Psalm 7:15-16; 33:10-11; 35:4-6; Isaiah 54:17; 2 Corinthians 10:4-5)*

**Plow Through:** to force a way through something violently. *(Judges 4:21; 5:26; Psalm 18:29)*

**Plunder:** to steal goods from a place or person, typically using force and during a time of war or civil disorder. *(Judges 5:30; Nahum 2:9)*

**Point of Prayer:** when prayer gears shift. One is no longer responsible for driving behind the wheel of prayer, but he or she is overtaken by the Holy Spirit and prays in the Spirit. This is when one shifts into another dimension or realm—when the intercessor abandons his or her personal prayer list and prays the will of God. Apostle Arome Osayi, Remnant Christian Network; Asuir, Nigeria

**Potter's Wheel:** a usually horizontal disk revolving on a vertical spindle and carrying clay. *(Jeremiah 18:1-4)*

**Pour out:** to cause a liquid to flow from a container into a cup or other vessel. *(Numbers 28:7; 2 Kings 9:6; Job 16:20; Joel 2:28; Acts 2:18)*

**Power:** might, strength, force. *(Luke 10:19; Acts 1:8)*

**Pray in the Spirit:** to pray in harmony with the will of God by speaking in a heavenly language only given by the Holy Spirit. *(Ephesians 6:18; Romans 8:26; Jude 20)*

**Preemptive Action:** an attack or strike that is intended to weaken or damage an enemy or opponent. *(Joshua 6;* Judges 3:12-25; *2 Samuel 5:19-20; Psalm 109)*

**Preserve:** to keep something as it is, especially to prevent it from decaying or to protect it from being damaged or destroyed. *(Genesis 45:5; 50:20; 2 Kings 19:34; Psalm 16:1; 25:20; 121:7; Proverbs 14:3; Ephesians 4:3)*

**Press and Release:** to press through or into prayer and release the burden.

**Prevail:** to prove more powerful than opposing forces; to be victorious; to gain control or influence. *(Deuteronomy 21:10; Psalm 21:8-11; 72:7; 94:15; Proverbs 19:21; Romans 8:37)*

**Pride:** self-respect or improper and excessive self-esteem (known as conceit or arrogance). Pride can be defined as elevating one's opinions and thoughts above God's authoritative Word. *(Psalm 73:6)*

**Prisoner of War:** a person who has been captured and imprisoned by the enemy. *(Judges 16:21-25)*

**Python:** The following is a listing of the natural characteristics of pythons: They are some of the largest snakes in the world. These big, nonvenomous snakes can range from 23 inches to 33 feet in length, and they can weigh anywhere from 7 ounces to 250 pounds. Pythons don't chase after their food because they are ambush hunters that can locate warm-blooded animals by using heat-sensing "pits" or holes along their jaw. It waits until the animal comes close, and then a python grabs the prey with its sharp, backward-curving teeth, coils its body around the prey, and squeezes tight. The snake is not trying to crush its prey; its goal is to stop its potential meal from breathing. After that, the python unfolds its flexible jaw, opens wide, and swallows its prey whole—usually headfirst—flexing and contracting its muscles to move the meal down its throat and into its stomach. Biblically, the original Greek word translated as "a spirit of divination" literally means "a spirit of Python." This spirit draws power from a demonic source and information about the future is revealed. This spirit of divination brings much profit by fortune-telling. *(Acts 16:16-18)*

# *Prayer Point*

*Father Lord, thank you for your good plans concerning my life. I thank you for your blessings upon my life, I thank you for it is your desire to settle me. Father, arise in Your divine power settle the issues concerning my life. Any powers assigned to divert my divine settlement, be roasted by fire in the name of Jesus. All due rewards, Father, by your power release them in the name of Jesus. Restore to me everything I have lost in the name of Jesus. I thank you in advance for your wondrous working power. Amen.*

# Q

**Quantum Leap:** a huge, often sudden, increase or dramatic advance in something (usually as it relates to time). *(Joshua 10:11-14; 2 Chronicles 20:15)*

**Quicken:** to make it more rapid: hasten, accelerate; "quickened her steps." Biblically, it means to bring it to life or restore it to its former flourishing condition; revive. *(Psalm 71:20; 85:6; 119:37; Isaiah 57:10; Romans 8:11)*

# *Prayer Point*

*Father, we ask You for the deep wells to open inside these Intercessor. Let the deep wells open, let their ears open to hear and respond to the call of prayer. We call them out, we call the intercessors forward, we call them forward in their distinct anointing and abilities in the name of Jesus. We ask you Lord to put a fire on them, a fire that cannot be consumed. We pray, Lord, for every intercessor all over the world that You touch them, recharge their bodies, give them the mind to intercede, give them the heart to pray it through, give them the burden to weep over it. Father, we thank you that you be removing every pitfall of insecurity, comparison, jealousy, every pitfall the enemy has constructed for their fall in the name of Jesus. We thank you for a new fire, a holy fire, a fresh fire upon them. Consuming fire, fall in the name of Jesus. (excerpt from The Intercessors Prayer, 2022)*

*—Apostle Yolanda Stith,*
*The Father's House of Baltimore*
*Baltimore, MD*

# R

**Rattlesnake:** As it grows, a rattlesnake sheds its skin. With each shed, it adds another segment to its rattle. The rattle segments interlock loosely, so when a snake wiggles its tail, they click and rattle against each other. You can't tell the age of a rattlesnake by counting the segments, though. A snake may shed more than once a year, and sometimes segments break off. A snake locates prey by scent, with the help of its tongue. The forked tongue flicks in and out, picking up odor particles. Then the snake lies in wait until its prey comes along. When prey comes close enough, the heat-sensitive pits on each side of a rattlesnake's head enable the snake to "see" a heat image of its prey. The snake lunges and strikes, injecting venom with its fangs. An alarmed snake usually tries to escape or hide, so be sure to stay out of its way. Rattlesnakes sometimes warn away predators by shaking their rattle. Biting is a last resort, but a snake may strike quickly if it is startled. So, be alert when you're hiking, and move away if you see a rattlesnake. Be careful where you put your hands and feet. Spiritually, "rattlesnake" may reflect underlying fears and anxieties that one is experiencing. It could signify a situation or relationship that is causing stress and unease. Rattlesnakes often represent hidden threats or deceitful individuals in your life. *(Psalm 58:3-9)*

**Rebellion:** the action or process of resisting authority, control, or convention—and it always begins in the heart. *(1 Samuel 12:15; Isaiah 14:12-14)*

**Recompense:** compensation or reward given for loss or harm suffered or effort made; restitution. *(Numbers 5:8; Ruth 2:12; Job 34:11; Isaiah 40:10; Lamentations 3:64; Matthew 16:27; 2 Thessalonians 1:6; Hebrews 10:30)*

**Recover:** to regain possession of/restore something stolen or lost. *(1 Samuel 30:8; 2 Samuel 8:3; Job 33:25; Jeremiah 8:22; John 5:9)*

Terri J. Davis

**Redeem:** to gain or regain possession of something in exchange for payment. *(Exodus 6:6; Ruth 4:3-4; 2 Samuel 7:23; Psalm 25:22; Lamentations 3:58; Galatians 3:13; Titus 2:14)*

**Redeeming the Time:** Time that is lost can be redeemed! If you are willing to exchange the hurt, discomfort, disappointment, lies, past issues, etc., then God will enable you to regain and recoup time that was previously squandered. *(Ephesians 5:16)*

**Reinforce:** to strengthen or support an object or substance, especially with additional material. *(1 Samuel 2:4; Ezra 5:9)*

**Rejection:** the act of pushing someone or something away. *(Leviticus 26:15; 1 Samuel 16:1; Psalm 51:11; John 3:18)*

**Release:** to set free from restraint, confinement, or servitude; to relieve from something that confines, burdens, or oppresses. *(John 8:36)*

**Release the Sound:** the act or an instance of liberating or freeing as from restraint; the act or manner of concluding a musical tone or phrase. *(Joshua 6:5; 2 Samuel 5:24; 1 Chronicles 15:19-29)*

**Remove the veil:** expose a truth that we have not yet seen. *(Jeremiah 13:26; Hosea 2:3; Ephesians 5:11)*

**Renewed Heart:** a heart cleansed from evil; a heart cleansed from pride; free to be holy, set apart for God, and to live a holy life led by the Holy Spirit. *(Psalm 51:10; Colossians 3:10)*

**Renounce:** to reject; declare one's abandonment of a claim, right, or possession. *(Matthew 16:24; Titus 2:12)*

**Repairer of the Breach** a person whose job is to repair things that are broken, ruptured, damaged, or in a torn condition. *(Isaiah 58:12)*

78

**Repent:** to turn from sin and be dedicated to Christ. *(Job 6:29; Psalm 4:4; Luke 13:5; Acts 3:19)*

**Request:** to ask for something; to ask as a favor or privilege. *(Philemon 6-7)*

**Rescind:** to revoke, cancel, or repeal a law, order, or agreement. *(Esther 8:3; Psalm 90:13)*

**Rescue:** to save someone from a dangerous or distressing situation; keep from being lost or abandoned; retrieve. *(Exodus 3:8; 1 Samuel 17:35; 2 Chronicles 32:11)*

**Resist:** to struggle or fight back when pressured or attacked. *(Joshua 8:10; James 4:7)*

**Resistance:** the refusal to accept or comply with something; the attempt to prevent something by action or argument. *(Ezekiel 44:6; Acts 26:14; 1 Corinthians 10:13)*

**Rest:** to relax into something and let it support you. *(Genesis 2:2-3; Psalm 4:8; 23:2-3; 62:1-2; 127:1-2; Proverbs 3:21-24; Jeremiah 6:16)*

**Restoration:** the returning of someone or something to a former condition, place, or position. *(Isaiah 58:8; Jeremiah 33:6; Acts 3:21; 2 Corinthians 5:19)*

**Restore:** to give something previously stolen, taken away, or lost back to the original owner or recipient. *(Genesis 20:7; Exodus 22:7; Deuteronomy 30:3; Nehemiah 5:11; Psalm 80:7; Jeremiah 30:17; Joel 2:25)*

**Reverse the effects of witchcraft:** to turn in the opposite direction, order, or position to where it started.

**Revoke:** to put an end to the validity or operation of a decree, decision, or promise. *(Esther 8:3; Psalm 90:13; Galatians 3:17)*

Terri J. Davis

**Root out:** to find and get rid of a harmful or dangerous person or thing. *(Exodus 34:24; Psalm 12:3; 34:16; Jeremiah 1:10; Micah 5:14)*

# *Prayer Point*

*Father, settle me this month in my finances and restore all my wasted years. Lord, reject all forms of rejection that have followed me and destroy every stronghold of failure assigned to my life. I decree and declare it is so in the name of the Lord Jesus. Pastor Blessing Olarewaju*

# S

**Safe:** protected from or not exposed to danger or risk; not likely to be harmed or lost. *(Genesis 6:19; Leviticus 25:18; Judges 6:23; 1 Samuel 14:23; 1 Kings 2:12; Nahum 1:7; John 17:12)*

**Satan:** His formal/official name is Lucifer, the prince of evil spirits and adversary of God (also known as the devil). He seduces humans into sin and falsehood. He is the ruler of darkness and hell is his home. Satan is seen as an agent subservient to God; therefore, he is NOT equal to God. He may be referred to as the Prince of Darkness, Beelzebub (Beelzebul), Mephistopheles, Baphomet, Lord of the Flies, the Tempter, the Antichrist, Father of Lies, and Moloch. *(Isaiah 14:12-15; Matthew 4:3; 12:24; 1 Peter 5:8; James 4:7)*

**Scepter of the Lord:** It is righteousness that He loves—His love demands righteousness. A scepter is a rod or staff adorned with gold and jewels that a king holds to indicate that he is in authority—the shepherd of his people. *(Psalm 110:2; Isaiah 14:5; Micah 7:14)*

**Seal up the hole in the pocket:** an admonishment for someone who never has cash (or someone who is a wasteful person). *(Haggai 1:6)*

**Seal up your victory:** to fasten or close securely; to prevent any form of entry from an enemy. *(Isaiah 8:16; Revelation 10:4)*

**Secure:** protect against threats; make safe; deliver (from); hide. *(Psalm 59:1; 64:2; Acts 26:17)*

**Seek:** to attempt or desire to obtain or achieve something. *(Jeremiah 29:13-14; Matthew 7:7)*

Terri J. Davis

**Shame:** a painful feeling that's a mix of regret, self-hate, and dishonor. Feeling shame—or being ashamed—is one of the most miserable feelings of them all. *(Isaiah 28:16; Zephaniah 3:19)*

**Shift(ed):** to move or cause movement from one place to another; change the emphasis, direction, or focus. *(Psalm 72; Romans 12:2; Colossians 3:2; Hebrews 12:2)*

**Shine your light:** to be a burning and shining light means that you're fervent, agile, and enthusiastic about spiritual things. It also refers to the light of God shining to expose darkness. *(Psalm 112:4; Matthew 5:16; John 1:5; 2 Corinthians 4:6)*

**Shout:** to utter a loud call or cry, typically as an expression of a strong emotion. *(Joshua 6:16; 1 Samuel 4:5; Ezra 3:12)*

**Shut the door:** It means "to close the door with a sudden, abrupt motion, firmly"—signifying that that part of your life is over.

**Sibling Rivalry:** competition between siblings especially for the attention, affection, and approval of their parents. It is also jealous of and harbor resentment toward one another. Some causes of sibling rivalry are lack of social skills, concerns with fairness, individual temperaments, special needs, parenting style, parent's conflict resolution skills and culture. *(Genesis 4; 25:19-34; 37)*

**Sickness:** the state or an instance of being sick; illness. *(Mark 1:34)*

**Sift(ed):** cause to flow or pass through a sieve; to scatter; to go through especially to sort out what is useful or valuable. *(Amos 9:9; Luke 9:31)*

**Silence the noise of the Enemy:** forbearance from speech or noise: muteness. *(Luke 4:35)*

**Sleep:** a state of reduced mental and physical activity. *(Psalm 4:8; Proverbs 3:24)*

**Smash into pieces:** to break to pieces with violence and often with a crashing sound, as by striking, letting fall, or dashing against something; shatter. *(Psalm 2:9; 107:16; Isaiah 30:31; Amos 6:11)*

**Snare:** to catch with a snare; entangle; to catch or involve by trickery. *(Psalm 35:7; 38:12; 91:3; Proverbs 6:2)*

**Snatch:** an act of snatching or quickly seizing something. *(John 10:28-29; Jude 23)*

**Song of the Lord:** a song the Lord sings over His people. *(1 Chronicles 25:7; Psalm 32:7; Zephaniah 3:17; Ephesians 5:19)*

**Songs of Deliverance:** public proclamations in honor of the Lord's love, justice, and deliverance. *(Psalm 32:7)*

**Sound the Alarm:** to warn people of danger; to awaken people to the reality of what lies before them. *(Isaiah 58:1; Ezekiel 33:6-9; Romans 2:21-23)*

**Spirit of Accident/Incident:** an undesirable or unfortunate happening that occurs unintentionally and usually results in harm, injury, damage, or loss; casualty; mishap: automobile accidents. Such an event resulting in injury that is in no way the fault of the injured person for which compensation or indemnity is legally sought. This spirit works often to keep one in a cycle of harm and mishap. People can overcome this spirit by declaring the Word of God over their lives, property, family, career, and ministry. *(Psalm 91:1-4)*

**Spirit of Anti-marriage:** a demonic goal to delay, rob, or destroy marriage covenants that are devoted to God. This spirit's work through witchcraft spells, which is to attack an individual's bloodline and cause one to live a life full of sorrow, disappointment, and regrets. If an individual achieves marriage, this spirit works to fuel conflict, anger, jealousy, diminished trust, insecurity, isolation, indifference and to ultimately drive a wedge between the spouses. To break free from this demonic stronghold, one must divorce this spirit by repenting, renouncing, and breaking anti-marriage curses and cycles in the family bloodline. Once can pray and declare the following:

*Father, I repent for the sin I have committed that opened the door to the anti-marriage spirit. I renounce and refuse to cooperate with any anti-marriage spells or curses. By the power and authority of the blood of Jeusu, I cancel and break every demonic covenant working in my bloodline. Cleanse and repair my family bloodline and make it as You originally intended it to be. All spiritual spouses, satanic wedding rings, spiritual weddings, blood covenants are destroyed by fire. May every plan of the enemy be made impotent. There will no longer be a delay of or sabotage of marriage because person You have destined for me shall see me. May it come quickly, and Your glory be the seal of approval in the name of the Lord Jesus. Amen.*

**Spirit of Delay:** something that causes deference, postponement, suspension, or pausing. The devil uses delay to distract, discourage, and destroy. The aim is to deny or deprive us of what we badly need to make our lives comfortable and happy. To overcome delay, pray for divine acceleration. God promised to bring about rapid expansion in Isaiah. King David prayed and asked God to deliver him speedily. We must pray and ask for divine guidance, divine assistance, and activation of our angels to clear demonic obstacles causing delay. We must ask the Lord to give us divine speed as He gave Elijah, who then ran faster than the king who was riding on the fastest chariot.

**Spirit of Fear:** The word fear in the Greek is *deilia* (di-lee-ah). This word means cowardice or timidity. A person with a spirit of fear or timidity may shy away from proclaiming the gospel or upholding the truth of God's word. This happens because of an impending sense of threat or danger whether it is real or imagined. One who is afraid of the consequences of their actions. This person becomes paralyzed and ineffective – not because they don't have power but because they stop taking action, because of fear. As believers there is this internal struggle happening, and Timothy was experiencing the same thing. If you focus on your abilities or the potential threat that can come from doing God's work, then fear or timidity will arise. However, if you are constantly being filled with the Spirit of God then he will help you overcome the spirit of fear. *(Acts 4:29; Ephesians 5:28; 2 Timothy 1:7)*

**Spirit of Heaviness:** a feeling of being dull, old, despondent, serious, and weighted down mentally. The spirit of heaviness should not be confused with clinical depression or mental illness. Spiritual heaviness is caused by a spiritual burden, which can only be remedied through spiritual means—while clinical depression and mental illness are considered physiological and psychological disfunctions. This spirit causes one to have a loss of appetite of God's Word and prayer, to shy away from other Believers, and to experience increased self-condemnation and bitterness toward the world. *(Isaiah 61:3)*

**Spirit of Limbo:** With this, one is in a situation where he or she seems to be caught between two stages and it is unclear what will happen next. This indicates the inability to go either way—one is somewhat stuck. *(Deuteronomy 30:19; Joshua 24:15; 1 Kings 18:21)*

**Spirit of Limitation:** restricts, restrains people's capability and can delay, de-rail, or destroy them so that they can't achieve or fulfill their preordained destiny in life. Spiritual limitations, also known as sympathetic magic, are inherited either through bloodline, curses, or sin. This spirit also affects one's physical health. *(Genesis 4; 27:37-40; Psalm 11:3; Luke 8:43-48; John 5:1-8)*

**Spirit of Offense:** a demonic spirit that can attach itself to someone that is holding on to negative emotions in his or her heart—like anger, bitterness, hate, pride, and especially unforgiveness. This spirit is rooted in pride. *(Proverbs 4:23; 6:16-19; 1 Peter 5:6)*

**Spirit of Procrastination:** something that causes the putting off of the commands of the Lord, which is the action of delaying or postponing obedience. The consequences of this sin are discontent and dissatisfaction. When we commit spiritual procrastination, God chastens us by allowing an unsettled heart of discontent and of feeling unfulfilled, no matter what we try in the world to satisfy us. It may appear a little thing, but in God's eyes procrastination is anything but little. May He help us to see how serious the sin of procrastination is not only in our lives but also in our fellowship with Him. *(Haggai 1:1-11)*

**Spirit of Polygamy:** exemplified in one who has been married multiple times and finds it difficult to stay married. Each marriage is short-lived due to feelings dissolving for the spouse, which finds one looking for another person to satisfy romantic feelings and desires. There's an infestation of fatherlessness, orphans, the ways of the vagabond, and hopelessness. This spirit is rooted in the bloodline through rejection, lust, addiction, adultery, fornication, and divorce. This spirit keeps one in a cycle of going from one relationship to another, leaving behind lovers who are emotionally wounded. This spirit causes one to make promises, vows, and agreements but not fulfill them (in all relationships)—family, business, friendship etc. The children born from these multiple marriages will find it difficult to maintain relationships and will repeat the same pattern as their polygamous parent. This spirit causes one to leave the presence of God to chase after his or her fleshly desires (the Bible calls them *strange women or men*). This spirit will bring one's life into endless marital harassment. *(Genesis 2:24; Exodus 21:10; Malachi 2:11; 1 Corinthians 7:2)*

**Spiritual Arrows:** signify invisible attacks from the powers of darkness to cause harm or untimely death in their victims. These arrows are invisible attacks from the kingdom of darkness to a specific person or target, which includes our businesses, marriages, or careers.

**Spiritual Dryness:** a feeling of being depleted or empty; a feeling far from the presence of God or having minimal or no spiritual growth. Some of the causes of spiritual dryness are lust, doubt, pride, and lack of prayer. *(John 4:3-14)*

**Spiritual Spouse:** A spiritual spouse *is a demon*. Demons can come into your life through open doors, such as the practice of witchcraft, horoscopes, astrology, and Ouija boards. A "spiritual spouse," or "spirit spouse," is a term used in shamanism. Spiritual husbands or wives help a shaman assist in their work of witchcraft. *(1 Timothy 4:1-3; 1 Peter 5:8-9)*

**Spoils of War:** property or goods of an enemy that are lawfully captured, seized, or confiscated in accordance with the laws of war; "plunder" (NIV). *(Numbers 31:9; 1 Chronicles 26:27; 2 Chronicles 20:25)*

**Stirring:** an initial sign of activity, movement, or emotion. *(2 Timothy 1:6)*

**Strange Fire:** fire that is foreign or unholy. *(Exodus 39:38; Numbers 3:4)*

**Strengthen the Inner Man:** It happens as we spend time studying and meditating on the Word, and praying in the spirit, in tongues. We also develop the right character and can do the things of God more effectively. *(Romans 7:22; Ephesians 3:14-16; Jude 20)*

**Strife:** violent or angry disagreement. *(Exodus 23:2; Deuteronomy 25:1; Psalm 55:9; 56:6; Proverbs 6:19; 10:12; 13:10)*

**Strong Deliverer:** Sovereign LORD—our strong deliverer—who shields our heads in the day of battle. *(Psalm 140:7)*

**Stronghold:** a place that has been fortified so as to protect it against attack; a place where a particular cause or belief is strongly defended or upheld. In the mind, Satan has established a lie in our thinking that we count as true but is a false belief. *(Psalm 9:9; 62:2; Ephesians 6:17; Romans 8:5; 2 Corinthians 2:10)*

**Strongman:** a strongman spirit is a high-ranking principality spirit. Strongmen sit on thrones in the spirit realm and rule over the evil, demonic spirits that operate in the earth realm. A strongman can gain access when there has been a door left open for the devil to gain access. When the enemy has gained entrance to a certain area, a strongman or a ruling spirit will be in control. Lesser evil spirits will follow as manifestations of the strongman, but to get rid of the evil spirits, we must first start at the root by dealing with the strongman. To be free from these strong men, deliverance must take place and one must bind the strongman and loose the Holy Spirit and warring angels. *(Mark 3:22, 27; Luke 11:21-22; John 12:31)*

**Strong Tower:** a central place in ancient cities to which people could run when facing danger and then find safety and protection. *(2 Samuel 5:9; Psalm 59:9; 62:5; Proverbs 18:10; Jeremiah 16:19)*

**Stumbling Block:** an obstacle to progress; an impediment to belief or understanding. Three major stumbling blocks are despair, laziness, and carelessness. *(Romans 14:13; 1 Corinthians 8–10)*

Terri J. Davis

**Succubus:** The female marine agents enchant men with sexual intercourse through the dream realm, causing uncontrollable masturbation urges and acts.

**Suddenly:** quickly and without warning; unexpectedly. *(Genesis 41:22; 1 Kings 18:7; Psalm 64:7; Isaiah 48:3; 51:5; Acts 16:26; Matthew 3:17)*

**Systems of the Human Body:** Organs of the human body are commonly grouped into thirteen systems. Each body system includes organs and structures that serve a common purpose. The systems are highly interdependent, working together to sustain life and enable interaction with the environment. *(Psalm 139:1; 1 Corinthians 12:12-26)*

> **Circulatory System:** a system of organs that includes the heart, blood vessels, and blood— which is circulated throughout the entire body of a human or other vertebrate. It includes the cardiovascular system, or vascular system, that consists of the heart and blood vessels. *(Leviticus 17:11; Matthew 9:20-22)*

> **Digestive System:** consists of the gastrointestinal tract plus the accessory organs of digestion. Digestion involves the breakdown of food into smaller and smaller components, until they can be absorbed and assimilated into the body. *(Matthew 15:17)*

> **Endocrine System:** a messenger system in an organism comprising feedback loops of hormones that are released by internal glands directly into the circulatory system and that target and regulate distant organs. In vertebrates, the hypothalamus is the neural control center for all endocrine systems. *(Psalm 139; Romans 7:14-23)*

> **Excretory System:** a passive biological system that removes excess, unnecessary materials from the body fluids of an organism, to help maintain internal chemical homeostasis and prevent damage to the body. *(Matthew 15:17)*

**Immune System:** a network of biological systems that protects an organism from diseases. It detects and responds to a wide variety of pathogens—from viruses to parasitic worms, as well as cancer cells and objects such as wood splinters, distinguishing them from the organism's own healthy tissue. *(Isaiah 28:15; Deuteronomy 7:15)*

**Lymphatic System:** an organ system in vertebrates that is part of the immune system, and complementary to the circulatory system. It consists of a large network of lymphatic vessels, lymph nodes, lymphoid organs, lymphoid tissues, and lymph. *(Psalm 68:35)*

**Muscular System:** an organ system consisting of skeletal, smooth, and cardiac muscles. It permits movement of the body, maintains posture, and circulates blood throughout the body. The muscular systems in vertebrates are controlled through the nervous system, although some muscles can be completely autonomous. *(Job 40:16)*

**Nervous System:** the highly complex part of an animal that coordinates its actions and sensory information by transmitting signals to and from different parts of its body. *(Proverbs 12:25; Isaiah 54:17; Matthew 6:25-27)*

# *Prayer Point*

*I overcome my accuser by the blood of Jesus and the word of my testimony which is the word of God, and I lay by life down as a living sacrifice unto the Lord. (Revelation 12:10-11) Father, let all demonic agents "be put to shame and brought to dishonor who seek after my life; let them be turned back and brought to confusion who plot my hurt" (Psalm 35:4). I cling to Your testimonies; O Lord, that I will not be put to shame! (Psalm 119:31). In the name of Jesus. Amen.*

# T

**Take advantage of:** make unfair demands on someone who cannot or will not resist; exploit or make unfair use of for one's own benefit. *(2 Corinthians 2:11)*

**Take back territory:** Isaiah 54:2-3 reads, *"Enlarge the place of your tent, and let them stretch out the curtains of your dwellings; do not spare; lengthen your cords and strengthen your stakes. For you shall expand to the right and to the left, and your descendants will inherit the nations, and make the desolate cities inhabited"* (NKJV). *(Numbers 33:53; 2 Kings 6:1-2; Psalm 2:8; Isaiah 11:11)*

**Territory:** an area of land under the jurisdiction of a ruler or state. *(Genesis 9:27)*

**Tested by Fire:** Everything we build here in life is going to go through two tests. They shall be tested by fire and water. Our faith will be like gold that has been tested in a fire. And these trials will prove that our faith is worth much more than gold that can be destroyed. *(Job 23:10; Isaiah 48:10; 1 Corinthians 3:11-15; 1 Peter 1:7)*

**Time Wasters:** hindrances and forces that make the journey of ten days become ten years or longer. This spirit wastes the time and age of men. It could come in any form or type, such as a plague, disease, or behavior. This spirit stops humans from achieving their full potential in life.

**Topple:** to become unsteady and fall. *(1 Samuel 5:1-4)*

**Transform:** to change in form, appearance, or structure; metamorphose. To change in condition, nature, or character; convert. *(2 Corinthians 5:17; Philippians 3:21)*

**Transgression:** the act of passing over or beyond; overpassing, as any rule prescribed as the limit of duty; the act of breaking or violating, as a law, civil or moral; the act of transgressing; the violation of a law or known principle of rectitude; breach of command; offense; crime; sin. *(Proverbs 17:11; Romans 4:15; Galatians 3:19; Hebrews 9:15)*

**Travailing Prayer:** The birth of a child is one of the most painful and exhausting processes, yet one of the most miraculous and sacred times in a woman's life—truly a time of awe and wonder. And, spiritually speaking, this is the experience that God uses to bless all who care and bear in prayer! It is when our hearts beat in union with God's heart. *(Luke 18:1-8)*

**Trespass:** an unwarranted or unlawful intrusion; sin. *(Proverbs 18:19; Matthew 6:14-15; Romans 3:23; 1 John 1:9)*

**Trial by Fire:** a test in which a person is exposed to flames in order to assess his or her truthfulness, commitment, courage, etc. *(1 Peter 1:7)*

**Twirl:** spin quickly and lightly around, especially repeatedly.

# *Prayer Point*

*Heavenly Father, help me unleash the power of prayer in my life. Show me how to make prevailing prayer a part of my life. For I know the Devil's python strategy is to stop or hinder my communication with You. Help me to be consistent, insistent, to have a continual life of prayer. I choose to grow closer to You in fellowship and relationship through prayer. In Jesus' name. Amen*

*—Pastor Jentezen Franklin*
*Free Chapel, Gainesville, GA*

# U

**Unbelief:** an absence of faith; refusing to believe in God and His Word. *(Matthew 17:19-21; Romans 11:23)*

**Uncover:** remove a cover or covering from; expose. *(Exodus 20:26; Proverbs 26:26; Lamentations 2:14)*

**Unity:** the state of being united or joined as a whole; same; agreement; no division. *(Psalm 133:1; Amos 3:3; Zechariah 11:7; Matthew 12:22-28; Romans 15:5; Ephesians 4:3)*

**Unravel:** to disengage or separate the threads; to cause them to come apart; to free from complication or difficulty; make plain or clear; solve!

**Unseat:** remove from a position of power or authority. *(Proverbs 25:5-15; Daniel 2:21)*

**Untangle:** to loosen from tangles or entanglement.

## *Prayer Point*

*Blood of Jesus, break asunder, rebuke, and make desolate every wicked program, plot in the heavens that would operate against me through the sun, moon, stars, and constellations in the name of the Lord Jesus.*

*—Apostle James Phred Kawalya*
*Lifeway Church of Christ*
*Kampala, Uganda*

# V

**Victim:** a person who suffers from a destructive or injurious action.

**Victory:** This is gained in defeating an enemy or opponent in a battle, game, or other competition. *(1 Chronicles 29:11; 1 Corinthians 15:57; 1 John 5:4)*

**Violate:** to fail to respect someone's peace, privacy, or rights. *(Ezekiel 22:26)*

**Violence:** the use of physical force to injure, abuse, damage, or destroy. *(Job 16:17; Ezekiel 22:26; Matthew 11:12)*

**Void:** to discharge, completely empty; to declare that something is not valid or legally binding.

# *Prayer Point*

*Father, thank You for redeeming the time and causing me to reap the benefits of recovering all that was lost, stolen, or broken. For Your mighty hand has reversed time and I shall come forth full of power and anointing. I am redeemed, my family is redeemed, my finances are redeemed, and I walk into the full of my assignment in the name of the Lord Jesus. Amen.*

# W

**Wait:** to remain inactive or in a state of repose, as until something expected happens. *(Joshua 1:9; Psalm 27:14; 37:7-9; Isaiah 40:31)*

**Waster:** This spirit has one agenda and that's to destroy. These demons cause us to waste our lives, attacking our talents, gifts, relationships, purpose, marriage, finances, etc. *(Isaiah 54:16)*

**Water:** the liquid that descends from the clouds as rain, forms streams, lakes, and seas, and is a major constituent of all living matter—and that, when pure, is an odorless, tasteless, very slightly compressible liquid oxide of hydrogen $H_2O$ which appears bluish in thick layers, freezes at $0°$ C and boils at $100°$ C, has a maximum density at $4°$ C and a high specific heat, is feebly ionized to hydrogen and hydroxyl ions, and is a poor conductor of electricity and a good solvent. Biblically, water is used as a symbol to show several different aspects of God's power. It can be used as a symbol of cleansing, as in the ceremonial washings of the Old Testament sacrificial system. Water represents the Word of God and sanctification. *(Exodus 30:18-21; Leviticus 16:4; 17:15; Ephesians 5:25-26)*

**Weight:** the amount or quantity of heaviness or mass; the amount a thing weighs. *(2 Corinthians 4:17-18)*

**Weight of Glory:** God has a glory that surpasses the glory of anything else in existence because He is of infinite value and worth. *(2 Chronicles 5:14; 2 Corinthians 4:17)*

**Wind of God:** The Holy Spirit comes in suddenly and from seemingly nowhere—*He whirls about the atmosphere and changes everything. (Hosea 13:15; Acts 2:2)*

**Winds of Change:** a term meaning that change is going to happen. *(Psalm 104:4)*

**Wisdom:** the soundness of an action or decision regarding the application of experience, knowledge, and good judgment. *(1 Kings 4:28-34; 10:1-14; Proverbs 21:30; 31:26; Ecclesiastes 7:19)*

**Witchcraft Embrace:** When a witch cannot touch us spiritually, the next attempt is to connect with us physically. When we see that their reach has become "friendly," it is the warfare that has increased.

**Works of the Flesh:** "Now the works of the flesh are evident, which are: adultery, fornication, uncleanness, lewdness, idolatry, sorcery, hatred, contentions, jealousies, outbursts of wrath, selfish ambitions, dissensions, heresies, envy, murders, drunkenness, revelries, and the like; of which I tell you beforehand, just as I also told you in time past, that those who practice such things will not inherit the kingdom of God" *(Galatians 5:19-21, NKJV)*.

**Workers of Darkness:** individuals who are on a demonic assignment to do the will of Satan. They also deny God as sovereign. *(Proverbs 4:14; Ephesians 5:11-14)*

**Workers of Iniquity:** evildoers or lawbreakers. *(Matthew 7:23)*

**Works of Darkness:** These have no beneficial use; they are unproductive and unfruitful, because they end in death. *(Romans 13:12-13)*

**Worship:** to show reverence and adoration for God; honor.

**Wound:** to inflict pain or cause an injury to someone physically, emotionally, or spiritually. *(Deuteronomy 32:39; Psalm 109:22; 147:3; Proverbs 1:16; Isaiah 53:5)*

**Wrestle:** to struggle with a difficulty or problem; to struggle, to strive, to contend in prayer and persevere through the hard place and overthrow one's opponent or put him or her off-balance. *(Ephesians 6:12)*

# *Prayer Point*

*I break loose and break free from witchcraft covens and evil altars in the name of the Lord Jesus. May every evil work backfire and return to the head of the sender. All witchcraft thrones around my territory be cast down and perish with all your summoning, in the name of the Lord Jesus. Amen.*

*—Apostle James Phred Kawalya*
*Lifeway Church of Christ*
*Kampala, Uganda*

# Y

**"Yes, Lord":** I will, I do, I agree. The more one matures in his or her relationship with God, the more that "Yes, Lord" becomes deeper and passionate. *(John 11:27)*

**Yield:** to surrender, submit, give way, give up, or relinquish possession of; offer (yourself). *(Romans 6:13)*

**Yoke:** a wooden crosspiece that is fastened over the necks of two animals and attached to the plow or cart that they are to pull; a part of a garment that fits over the shoulders and to which the main part of the garment is attached, typically in gathers or pleats. *(Galatians 5:1)*

## *Prayer Point*

*Father, In the name of Jesus Christ, I pray that the faith of Your people would be strengthen. Faith comes from hearing Your Word; so, Father, expand our revelatory knowledge of Your word so that our faith produces miracles, signs, and wonder like those of the Bible days. Your Word is true, and it will accomplish what You send it out to do. Father, help our unbelief so that we do not turn away from the kingdom assignments You have set before us. In the book of Luke, as Jesus prayed for Simon, I pray that our faith does not fail; rather it develops to believe that the impossible can become possible. Increase our capacity to believe in Your written and spoken Word and to never doubt. Amen.*

*—Psalmist Devena Witherspoon*
*Lebanon, TN*

# Z

**Zeal(lous):** dedication, passion, or enthusiasm for something. often used in a religious sense, meaning devotion to God or another religious cause, like being a missionary. Zeal doesn't have to be religious, though: a feeling of gusto and enthusiasm for anything can be called zeal. *(Numbers 11:25; 25:13; 2 Kings 19:31; 1 Corinthians 14:12; Titus 2:14)*

**Zen:** refers to a blend of yoga and Zen — religious teachings and practices. *(Exodus 20:3)*

**Zenith:** The sun reaches its zenith when it is as high in the sky as it is going to go on that day. *(Joshua 10:13; Habakkuk 3:11)*

**Zin:** silk thread twisted together, a fabric of the same. Synonyms: desire, appetite; intention, lust and trek.

**Zodiac:** an imaginary band in the heavens centered on the ecliptic that encompasses the apparent paths of all the planets and is divided into 12 constellations or signs each taken for astrological purposes to extend 30 degrees of longitude. *(Psalm 8:3; 19:1; 147:4).*

**Zodiac Sign:** refers to one of 12 specific constellations of the zodiac that the sun passes through. A person's particular sign of the zodiac is the one that the sun was in when they were born. It is a belief in astrology that a person's personality can be predicted using their sign of the zodiac. These signs are also known as horoscopes, in which the Lord condemns the astrologers of Babylon to judgment through the prophet Isaiah. Daniel puts these professional astrologers to shame when he interprets the king's dream through his reliance on God. Those who practice the work of astrology seek to replace the role only God can fill in our lives. It is a distraction from the Lord and His purpose for us and it serves as an introduction to spiritual forces of evil who seek to destroy you. *(Deuteronomy 18:10-14; Leviticus 19:31; Isaiah 47:13-14; Jeremiah 27:9; Daniel 2:27-28)*

**Zombie:** a will-less and speechless human (as in voodoo belief and in fictional stories) held to have died and been supernaturally reanimated. *(Zechariah 14:12)*

**Zoom:** to move or travel very quickly. *(1 Kings 18:45-46)*

# *Prayer Point*

*I Declare God's redemptive work through Jesus Christ, will come in new fullness of my life. "For you shall not go out with haste nor go by flight; for the Lord will go before you, and the God of Israel will be your rear guard!" I shall wait for the Lord. My feet will be put in His perfect timing. I shall recover all that has been lost and I am restored in the name of Jesus. My prayers are ordered, and the Lord shall order my feet.*

*—Apostle Chuck D. Pierce,*
*Glory of Zion International Ministries*
*Corinth, TX*

# REFERENCES

- Bible Study Tools, biblestudytools.com, 2024

- Blessing, Olarewaju, The Weapon of Prayer for Freedom from Captivity, Feb 2024, https://sotivation.com/the-weapon-of-prayer-for-freedom-from-captivity/

- Femrite, Tommi; Alves, Elizabeth; Kaufamn, Karen, Nov 2000, Intercessors: Discover Your Prayer Power

- GotQuestions.com, 2002-2024, Got Questions Ministries.

- King James Bible Dictionary, 2022, https://kingjamesbibledictionary.com

- Scriptures take from King James Version (NKJV), Public Domain

- Merriam-Webster.com Dictionary, Merriam-Webster, https://www.merriam-webster.com/dictionary/heal

- San Deiago Zoo, https://sdzwildlifeexplorers.org/animals/

- Scriptures take from New King James Version (NKJV), 1982, Thomas Nelson

# Notes

www.ingramcontent.com/pod-product-compliance
Lightning Source LLC
Chambersburg PA
CBHW052116020426
42335CB00021B/2784